JEMS
FROM JOHNSON

JEMS FROM JOHNSON

A Guide to Successful Customer Relationship Management

CLAUDE JOHNSON

iUniverse, Inc.
New York Lincoln Shanghai

Jems from Johnson
A Guide to Successful Customer Relationship Management

iUniverse books may be ordered through booksellers or by contacting:

iUniverse
2021 Pine Lake Road, Suite 100
Lincoln, NE 68512
www.iuniverse.com
1-800-Authors (1-800-288-4677)

ISBN: 978-0-595-42261-6 (pbk)
ISBN: 978-0-595-86597-0 (ebk)

Printed in the United States of America

The gem cannot be polished without friction, nor man perfected without trials.

(Chinese proverb)

Contents

Introduction

You might ask how I arrived at the point where I wanted to publish a book about Customer Relationship Management in the retail industry. Let's see if we can answer that.

Let's first address the size of the effort to write a book.

When I was in high school (oh, so many years ago), my English teacher would assign papers of 1,000 words or 1,500 words. I would hand in 1 page. She would ask where the rest of the assignment was. I said, "I have said what I want to say, short and sweet." The papers were punctuated properly and spelled correctly but did not meet the word count required. Fortunately or unfortunately, she did not flunk me.

With that experience or lack thereof in creative writing, I proceeded to the Military Academy at West Point. In freshman English, I came as close to flunking out of West Point as any cadet ever did who graduated. Fortunately again, the army likes short and sweet. However, I was afraid of writing lengthy papers and still am. Can you imagine the nightmares I would have had to write 150–200 pages of content?

In early 2001, I had a little time on my hands and decided there was a need for a newsletter that addressed all the statistics of database marketing; what are the statistics, why one would want to acquire the statistics, how to acquire the statistics, and what one would do with the statistics. It would be a free, bi-weekly, electronic newsletter (short and sweet—you may have heard that above). It would be case study driven, 2 to 3 or 4 pages with actual data from my clients. So, for the last several years, every 2 weeks, I have been publishing this short and sweet newsletter entitled *Jems from Johnson*. The subject matter changes every 2 weeks, which I love. I can quickly and with very few words, discuss a subject that is of interest to retail marketers. Sometimes I wonder about subject matter and a client will call about a problem, and bingo. An hour later a new edition of *Jems from Johnson* has been written, edited by my wife, and distributed to over 800 retailers.

Every edition is an actual case study from a client. It may focus upon a subject matter that is not universally accepted or needed. However, it addresses subject matter that most retailers have to face at some time whether they know it or not. If they do not address these issues head-on, profits are lost, opportunities are lost, sales are lost, or efficiencies are lost without the knowledge of the retailer. Every edition generates a few comments from retailers with thanks for validating their efforts or thanks for providing them with a method to solve a problem or thanks for shining a light on the unknown aspects of CRM.

"Does he <u>have</u> retail experience?" you ask!

In 1973, having spent 4 years at West Point and 5 years in the active army, I thought I would like to expand my horizons as a civilian.

I began talking to many people in many diverse industries. After such an exhaustive search, I was speaking to my dear wife. She said, "You've been trained in killing and maiming, why don't you try retail." So, I joined *Lane Bryant* (a big women/ tall women's retailer) in Indianapolis in the computer department. Having taught data processing/systems analysis for 2 years in the army, I was somewhat prepared for retail data processing.

Don't think I am a technician. Far from it. I never got the bug for the bits and bytes of data processing. I have enough programming and systems analysis to be very dangerous. My tenure in the army and the first couple of years at Lane Bryant were enough for me to know how to use technology as one of many management tools. I have learned that most people will make the right decision given the right information. Technology helps provide the right information faster and usually more accurate.

Since I never expected to be a computer nerd, I got out of data processing as quickly as I could (3 years after joining Lane Bryant). Because of my knowledge of technology and desire to get out of data processing, I was offered the position of Area Operations Manager in Los Angeles, an area that had 26 stores. Here we have a country boy from Boone, NC, recently out of the army, after 3 years of data processing, named to be the Area Operations Manager over 26 stores. Did I *ever* have a lot to learn!

I was a quick enough study that I was promoted a year later to Western Region Operations Manager over 52 stores (everything west of the Mississippi). Since I needed to visit every store during each season, "If it's Tuesday, this must be Belgium" (replace Belgium with Boulder!) comes to mind.

By the way, at the same time, during this Regional learning experience, I was heading up a pilot distribution center on the west coast processing Asian imports serving all stores east of Los Angeles. [Very heavy data processing support required.] Just in case you have not figured it out, all of Lane Bryant's stores, over 200 are east of Los Angeles!

These 2 years were a great learning experience. All of the people in the region and the distribution center were my teachers. They did not mind telling me what their responsibility was and what needed to be done to help them do it. I learned how merchandising impacted the distribution center, how distribution impacted inventory in the stores, how advertising/marketing yelled at the customers, how the store personnel are on the front lines (notice the military term), and how management had to get out of the way of the staff so they could do their job. I could not have ordered a better experience for the 2 years in this position. One senior executive in the company explained the sense of urgency to process merchandise thru the distribution center as "imagine these dresses as fresh fruit. Every day they stay in the distribution center is another day they rot." Fortunately, we did not have too many dresses rotting in the distribution center.

Lane Bryant apparently liked what I was doing enough to call me back to the home office in NY to head up the new national distribution center and network. How does someone running a distribution network get into marketing? Stay tuned. I had a great 10 year run with Lane Bryant. The experience of having worked for a large specialty retailer in all the varied positions gave me knowledge that I did not appreciate at the time. But leaving Lane Bryant was the best thing that ever happened to me.

The next chapter in Claude's retail experience was at NBO Menswear, a specialty, discount retailer in the NY metro area and Washington, DC. As Executive Vice President, Chief Administrative Officer, I directed all the admin functions as well as MIS (data processing had been renamed *Management Information Systems* by this time) and the distribution network. For each of the subordinate functions, I was fortunate to have very skilled individuals who taught me a great deal about menswear retailing. Since I tend to be someone who nudges into places where I have not been invited, I was able to influence a great deal of the store, merchandising, and advertising functions. My wife, Tina, said that I was Vice President of **Other**. [Everything that no one else wanted was mine.] Fortunately, each function came with an experienced leader.

During this time, my Vice President of Distribution identified some excess space in the distribution center and suggested that he and I should create a company to process other retailer's overflow ticketing and distribution. Sounded like a good idea. We created Priority Distribution as a subsidiary company of NBO Menswear. It generated a great deal of high margin revenue for the company because the fixed costs were covered by the distribution required for NBO Menswear. This very successful effort turned the entrepreneurial light on.

So, after twenty years in retail, where's the retail *marketing* experience?

First remember that most of my hands on experience in retail has been in operations functions like store operations and physical distribution. But I did have a rather extensive background in data processing and the use there of. [Database marketing by definition is heavily influenced by technology.] With that knowledge, let's discuss an event that was the jumping off point in my marketing experience.

The president of NBO Menswear had a great marketing idea. "Let's have a sweepstakes and the prize will be a BMW. Claude, you take care of all the admin associated with collecting the entry blanks and keying them into a customer database. The reason we are doing this is so we can build a list of customers to mail to."

Sounds simple until: we received over 100,000 entry forms! There were duplicates galore. We had no way of knowing if the person on the form had even made a purchase. We also determined that even if we built a database and mailed the customers, we had no structure to measure results. We ended up throwing all the forms out. But we still wanted to acquire the names of our customers so we could mail them.

One day, while walking thru the accounting office, I saw 10 ladies balancing credit card slips from the stores. I looked at all those credit card slips and mused, "Wouldn't it be wonderful if we knew who all those customers were? (Would we not love their name/address information)?" Since we had just had a presentation from one of the credit card companies trying to help us in marketing, I thought they should be able to give us the names/addresses of our credit card customers.

So, off I went. I called the presenter from the credit card company and he said it was impossible. He said to check with one of the credit bureaus.

So, off I went. I called one of the credit bureaus and asked "if I give you the credit card number from one of my customer's transactions, can you give me the name/

address back?" He said no. So I called another person at the same credit bureau and asked the same question. He said, "You know, I'm not sure. Let me check and I'll get back to you."

A few weeks later, he told me that they had never done this before but they could do it and would have to write some programs.

So, off I went. While the programs were being written by the credit bureau, I worked with my VP of MIS to begin the construction of a customer database to receive information back from the credit bureau. I was so fortunate that my VP of MIS saved everything. He had credit card records going back to the civil war. (I know they dealt in actual money then!) We cut off the last 2 years, included all the company executives' card numbers for validation and sent the file off to the credit bureau. In a couple of weeks, we received back the names/addresses of about 75% of those we had sent out. We loaded the database, back loaded all the transactions we had for these customers (thus the benefit of the VP of MIS saving the transactions), printed a postcard and mailed 400,000 customers. We generated over $1.4 million (back when $1.4 million was a lot of money) in incremental sales for our first direct mail piece ever at NBO. Remember, the database had been created overnight with 2 years of sales transactions with no manual effort and a side benefit (very large impact) was that the customer's future purchases could be tracked by the credit card number. No one believed it but I knew we had a tiger by the tail.

All of my retail experience came to bare on this thing called *database marketing* now known as **CRM** (*Customer Relationship Management*). Everything we did after that first direct mail piece was tested and measured to the nth degree. I loved the aspect of proving to the CFO who was a non-believer that all of this was working. Like every other CFO, he believed the customers would have come in without the cost of database marketing.

I became obsessed with learning more and more about all aspects of CRM. I said to myself, if I can do this for NBO Menswear, I can do this for other retailers. Remember, the entrepreneurial bug hit me with Priority Distribution. I started, with 2 partners, a database marketing outsource company named Retail Resources. It was all based on the acquisition of name/address via the process that became known as *credit card reverse append*. The client base grew from a few retail chains to over 40 plus some restaurant chains and resorts.

You know, you wake up one day and you are no longer a retailer. You are a database marketer. I can safely say that I am not a good **marketer**, but I am a **very good database marketer.**

Now.... back to the book.

You know if you write 3–4 pages every 2 weeks, after a couple of years you have enough pages for a book. The newsletter, *Jems from Johnson*, was the perfect vehicle for me. It is short and sweet about a current subject of interest to those on the distribution list. We just needed to organize, rewrite a few *Jems* and edit the material. **Voila, the book!**

In this book, you will discover methods to save millions of dollars in your CRM efforts if you are a large retailer or thousands if you are a small retailer. You will discover suggestions for increased profit using common sense methods that have been proven over and over with my client base. You will discover methods to grow your customer base, nurture your customers, and reap the rewards of some hard work. Just like the farmer who plants in the fall and reaps the rewards in the spring.

Each Chapter and Sub-Chapter discusses a topic, short and sweet. Read a chapter before each of your Monday Executive Meetings and see how it can impact your customer relations.

Enjoy your reading.

Chapter I

January—Customer Identification

First some history: How did CRM become CRM? We begin with:

1. Direct Mail (actually mailing to someone other than PRESENT OCCUPANT);

2. Target Marketing (using demographics to presume that this household might, in fact, may have interest in your offer);

3. Customer Specific Marketing (CRM's parent, where honing offers to customer was key);

4. CUSTOMER RELATIONSHIP MANAGEMENT: early educators had it right. The "<u>R</u>'s" are the most important letter in learning: readin', 'ritin', 'rithmetic, and RELATIONSHIP. We "read" our customer's needs; "write" to maintain their loyalty; use "arithmetic" (statistics) to determine who our BEST customers are and then build a "relationship" as we: COMMUNICATE, COMMUNICATE, COMMUNICATE!

(Wk 1: Is there a *resident* in the house?)

What is the most difficult aspect of Customer Relationship Management in the retail industry?

- Is it counting all the money we make by treating our customers right?

- Is it deciding to do Customer Relationship Management (CRM) in the first place?

- Is it determining what the offer on a mail piece should be?

- Is it picking the right customers to whom to mail this great piece?

None of those things can even become a problem until we solve the most difficult problem of all: How do we identify the customer, or get the customer to identify him or herself, at the point of purchase?

Customer identification is the most difficult aspect of CRM in the retail industry, bar none.

Historically, retail transactions were anonymous. Customers came in, bought stuff (we hope), paid for it (we hope), and left—all without telling us who they were. But to perform CRM, we need customers to identify themselves. This is what allows us to:

1. **Communicate** with the customers after they leave
2. Track their purchases
3. Employ all the CRM bells and whistles that we'll describe later in this tome.

Is this selfish on our part? A little. But there must be something in it for the customer as well. Without that benefit to the customer, none of our CRM initiatives will work.

Some companies try to solve the problem by instituting a card-based, loyalty program. This is a good idea for many retailers, as customers must identify themselves during each transaction, in order to get the bennies of the program. However, it's not a panacea. Only a portion of our customers will join the loyalty program. What will we do about the rest of them?

Some companies have modified their private credit card system for more effective customer marketing. Unfortunately, most customers aren't looking for another credit card. The balance of retailers has a very difficult row to hoe. For those of you not from the South, that means: it's no piece of cake.

Of course, it might be quite easy for a professional sales associate to identify some customers at the point of sale. After all, the seller should recognize the customer who spent $1000 in the store last week.

Sorry. Not good enough. That customer identification must translate into something a computer can use to track the customer—only then is the customer identified in our system. Only at this point can we track sales, **communicate** information to the customer, and hope to impact future sales.

We need to enter that identification into the POS register with each transaction, so that it can be attached to the sales transaction. Without this information in our database, we will lose contact with our customers as soon as they leave the store.

As we start the New Year, let's take the challenge head-on. There is no perfect answer to the problem of customer identification. Most retailers attack it from multiple directions, using every method available. Multiple talents and experiences are needed to ferret out all the possibilities for capturing the customer's identity, and for making sure that each sales transaction gets properly posted to the customer's account.

What won't help us on this mission is the one thing we have plenty of: excuses. Here are a few favorites:

Excuse #1: *New Yorkers are different and don't like to give name and address.*

Fuhgeddaboudit! I've lived in the NY metro area for 25 years. Just like every other red-blooded American, I will give my name and address—if there's a reason to do so. The possibility of saving money is one such reason, and a very persuasive one. There isn't a New Yorker alive who wants to pay full retail!

Excuse #2: *Californians won't give their name to anyone they don't trust.*

Then we better start engendering trust. Let's explain how the information will be used and why it's advantageous to the customer to provide it. Then we better keep our promise to use the information only for the stated reasons. For any aspiring politicians out there, the "keep your promise" bit will sound foreign. But try!

Excuse #3: *It causes a line to back up at the register.*

We should have such problems. A retailer once told me, "I like there to be a line at the register. Makes it look like something is happening—a buzz going on." Naturally, there are times when a long line will justify not asking for name and address. But it's far less often than we might think.

Excuse #4: *It's sale time and these are different customers than my full price customers.*

Give me a break! Just because someone buys an item at a reduced price, it doesn't mean he or she won't be there to buy our new, full price merchandise. My dear wife will buy at any price—markdown, full, or double-full. Thankfully, she does draw the line at triple-full price.

Excuse #5: *The transaction was only for $10.*

Let's learn this once and for all. Customers don't always spend gobs of money. Sometimes they buy a single item for $10. Other times, they will spend $500. We want to track all those transactions, even the little ones. Multiple transactions increase frequency, which is one of the major metrics in CRM. Even a small transaction can improve recency, another important CRM measurement.

Excuse #6: *The customer lives in California—not my customer.*

Hey dude! There are a couple of problems with this:

(a) If you're just ringing the sale, how can you tell the customer lives in California? Was it the Beaujolais or the Blueberry color hair?

(b) We have a store in California, too. If we capture the name and address, we could invite the customer to that store.

(c) Even if we don't have a store in California, we should be promoting our direct channels of catalog and web, for which customer location is almost irrelevant.

I recently spoke with a friend who runs a one-store chain in Philadelphia. He has customers all over the country, even in California. Just because someone is from California or another foreign country, we can't forget to ask for name and address. We might find a lot of California customers shopping at our funky store, and decide to open a West Coast store to service them.

Excuse #7: *I asked 5 customers in a row for their name and address. They all said "no".*

When asking customers to identify themselves, we can't have thin skin. We will receive plenty of rejections. We need to keep on truckin'. You can rehearse in the mirror: "I will continue to request information … I will continue to request information!"

Excuse #8: *I asked her if she wanted to be on our mailing list and she said "no".*

Would we want to be on someone's "mailing list"? Only wacko people want to be on a "mailing list". Nevertheless, people do want to receive special offers available only to our "best customers". They do want to receive information relevant to their preferences; they want to be the first to know when that fall jacket arrives.

I'm often asked: What is a normal capture rate of customer information at POS? There is no normal rate. Every retail format is different (department stores, specialty stores, outlet stores, electronics, grocery stores, etc). Each retailer determines how much effort and expense to put into capturing customer information. Some retailers don't even understand why it's important.

My Suggestion:

> **Find out where you are today. Determine if your current capture of customer information is sufficient to build a successful CRM program.**

If there is a gap in your information capture, set reachable goals for the stores over the next few months. Monitor the success of the stores, and the associates in those stores. Remember, you can't change something that you didn't measure. Take corrective action where necessary. Then raise the bar, and monitor the success again.

Will we ever capture the name and address for everyone who purchases? We probably won't, unless we're selling homes. I used to say that I would sell my firstborn to be able to identify customers at POS. At the time, I would have given him away. Now he's the father of my grandson and granddaughter, and I wouldn't part with either him or them. In the real world, less than a 100 percent capture rate is acceptable. You must set your own realistic goals.

In the year ahead of us, we have an opportunity to start to move the meter. In the next few weeks, we will look at several methods of identifying the customer at the point of sale, and the statistics associated with that effort. Today, let's begin by making our #1 problem our #1 priority. We need to know:

"Who Is My Customer?"

My father said, "Heaven isn't reached in one day." I happen to believe he is in heaven—but I know he was right. It doesn't happen in one day. The sooner that we start, the further we'll get.

(Wk 2: Reach and touch someone)

Last week, we diagnosed what ails us: the ever-vexing problem of getting custom-ers to identify themselves at the point of purchase. Without that elusive name and address, we can't thank the customer for the purchase, give a special discount, or inform the customer about new product arrivals and sale events. If we're missing that information, then we've lost control of our own destiny. Inquiring minds want to know:

"Who Is My Customer?"

While we're at it, we also need to know how to get in touch, via mail, email or telephone. Further, we must be able to match sales to the customer's historical record. "Hey, aren't you the guy with the funny shirt who bought the 3-way adap-tor last Thursday?" may show a certain gift for identification. But it doesn't do much for our computer data files.

In order for our computer systems to do their work accurately, we need a num-ber—a number that can represent the customer. That number might be the home telephone number. Customers already know it from memory. Other members of the family know it. Customers are accustomed to providing it in retail situations. Here is a 10-digit number the computer can use as an identifier, in order to track the customer's purchase history.

Problem solved? Not quite. Where will the name and mailing address come from? We could ask the customer for a name, address, city, state, and zip code at every transaction. I can hear the customer now: "I come in here every day and you ask me the same question. Can't you make this easier?"

Of course, we can. With only the telephone number, we can identify the customer from transaction to transaction. But we can't send a postcard to a telephone num-ber. Now, we want to go one step further, to third party companies (data provid-ers) who will take the telephone number, and return to us the name and address associated with that number. Without further ado, I give you:

Telephone Reverse Append

If we are looking for one telephone number at a time, we could use the Internet lookup facilities provided by a variety of different companies. But if we need to look up thousands of telephone numbers, we should send the file of telephone numbers to a company able to run multiple numbers at one time. This third party provider will return to us the names and addresses that correspond to the phone numbers submitted. If we sell to more than one customer a day, this is the process we would use.

What is the cost for this facility? Would you believe that it's only a few pennies per record? (This assumes a minimum job charge of a few hundred dollars. The intent of this minimum job charge is to eliminate companies who would require a whole job set-up for ten phone numbers.)

Let's look at some statistics. Below are the numbers for a reverse append process from one of my clients; this client sends numbers out to a third party data provider on a monthly basis. The cost for this process would be approximately $6600, or .07 cents per name.

95,168	Telephone numbers sent
39,725	Records where the name/address was reverse appended
41.74%	Hit rate

Warning: The hit rate does not refer to Kasey Kasem's Top Forty Countdown. It's not a tally of participants in the Soprano Family early retirement program. The hit rate indicates the number of successful matches between telephone number, name and address.

This hit rate can vary markedly, depending on the accuracy of the data entry at point of purchase, the number of customers who have entered their number on a telephone suppression list, the prevalence of private or unlisted numbers, or even different regions of the country. Even the manner in which a phone number is requested can affect the accuracy of the information that is obtained. Some customers will provide bogus information simply to get a salesperson off their back.

Is it worth the hassle of asking for a phone number, if only 41.74% of the requests result in a name and address that can be put on the customer database and tracked? Let's consider:

In the above example, if by asking for phone number instead of full name/address, we saved one minute on each transaction for which we obtained a telephone number, we would have saved 923 hours on the 95,168 transactions at the point of sale. If we are paying $10 per hour, we saved $9,230 dollars of payroll. If, instead, we had forms for customers to complete in the store, then we sent those forms to a data entry firm at 16 cents each, we would have spent an additional $3,500. (I know—it sounds like "If train A leaves Station A at 8 AM and travels at 50 miles an hour to Station B, at what time will …")

Here's the best part. With the telephone reverse append, we were able to create 39,725 new customer records. Previous sales now can be back loaded and attached to a particular customer. If the customer continues to give the same phone number, then all future purchases can be tracked. Is there anything better?

Imagine what we could do with this information. If you can't imagine—call me. That's how I make my living. Some of the companies with whom I work will even admit that I helped a little. Now that we know who our customer is, we can **communicate** to them!

Let's say we were to mail these 39,725 customers an average of five times over their lifetime (a reasonable average for the total). Assuming an average response rate of 5% (retailers average better response), and an average transaction of $50, we would generate almost $500,000 in sales. Most retailers would see that as an acceptable Return on Investment for a cost of $6,000.

I admit when I first heard of this crazy little thing called "telephone reverse append", my first reaction was "Yeah, right." I did enjoy saying "reverse append, reverse append", though. Over time, I discovered that it makes a lot of sense (also cents). It is the least-expensive option for customer identification available to retailers with numeric-only registers (yep, they're still out there) quickly entered at POS, with a generally high degree of accuracy. It is viable even if you don't have a register. It merely requires entry of 10 digits on a 3x5 card for tracking. There's a coffee shop in Melbourne, Florida that keeps track of their loyal customers on an index of 3x5 cards, using the telephone number as the key to the file.

Best of all, when necessary, it can be used in lieu of any other methods. What if a husband is purchasing, but the wife has the loyalty card in her purse? The husband could still provide his home phone number, and the transaction could be credited accurately to his household record. Even retailers using other means of customer identification can continue to utilize this method, at least in part.

For those retailers still not doing anything to identify the customer or track purchase history …

My Suggestion:

   You better do something!

There are many ways to persuade customers to raise their hands and identify themselves at the point of purchase. (None of them includes free dishes for the customer.) The telephone reverse append process is a very good place to start.

I now have one client whose entire customer base, more than 1.4 million shoppers and their purchase histories, has been created via telephone reverse append. That's called hitting the mother lode in retail CRM.

(Wk 3: "TLC"—Transactions Love Customers)

Do you think we've solved the retailer's riddle:

"Who Is My Customer?"

Not so fast. As handy as the telephone reverse append may be, it only covers one of many scenarios for uncovering a customer's identity. Given the customer's telephone number, we've seen how we can circle back and, with the help of our friendly third-party data provider, uncover the customer's identity from ten simple digits. Now, let's add a new twist:

What if the number we have isn't a phone number at all? What if the only number we have is the credit card number?

Let's imagine that we are a retailer ready to leap into the 21st Century. After all, **WE ARE** a retailer ready to leap into the 21st Century. Suppose we have a private credit card system, managed by a bank. This house card produces 20 percent of our sales. Another 60 percent of our business comes via third party credit cards. The balance is cash/check and other miscellaneous objects of art.

The Breakdown:

20%	House Credit Card
60%	Third Party Credit Cards
20%	Cash/Check

Of course, we know the identity of the people using our own private credit card. Unfortunately, there are not many people in that category. In most cases, very few of our customers use the store credit card. In all likelihood, that 20 percent of sales comes from only 10 percent of our customers.

Over the years I've kept a collection of my old credit cards. Buried in a small bureau drawer, there are plastic cards from long gone stores like Korvette's and Orbach's. Most of the cards I never used more than once. Still, it's fun to open up that drawer every once in awhile, for a brief round of retail nostalgia. My artifacts require a lot less space than a collection of old license plates.

But how about those other customers—the ones using third party credit cards, and contributing 60 percent of our sales? If only we knew who they were, we could **COMMUNICATE** to the customer and we could:

- Tell them about new offerings
- Reward the good guys
- Identify those who are about to stop shopping

It sets a CRM guy's mouth to watering. What our world needs now is a little TLC.

Okay, that's not the real name of this process. It stands for Transactions Love Customers—and I made it up, as if you didn't know. But the process, while relatively new, is very real. It can be provided by several reliable third-party data providers, and is more complex than it looks on the surface. The name itself should give you the basic idea. We're working backward here, using the transaction to track down the customer after the fact. Are you with me? Let's get on the trail …

First, in order for **TLC** to do its job, we need to narrow the playing field. The process starts with an analysis of our current customer file, in this case the house credit file, to identify the market area around each of our stores. By ranking the zip codes in descending customer count, for those customers patronizing the store, **TLC** can then perform a demographic analysis to profile our store's customer.

Once this profiling is done, **TLC** is ready to search the transaction records that we have, even those with only a credit card number, to determine who our customer is.

The good news is: When a credit card is swiped through the magnetic card reader, the magnetic stripe provides us not only with the credit account number, but also with the name (last, and usually the first). During the transaction, we should ask for the customer's zip code. This is only five digits, and the customer will almost always provide it. Have you ever been asked for your zip code? What did you think the retailer was doing with it?

Every night, when the register is polled, our point of sale register transmits the name and zip code to the home office. This means that for each credit card transaction, in addition to the purchase information, we have a credit card number, a name, and a zip code.

The bad news is: This still doesn't fully answer our question. It doesn't adequately identify the customer. We can't **communicate** to a name and a zip code. That's why we need a little **TLC**. If we send a name and zip code to **TLC**, it will search the zip code for that name. TLC has over 200 million consumers in their US database.

Let's say that we're looking for a "Claude Johnson" (and what retailer isn't?). TLC will search the zip code we've provided, to find that name. If the name is found in the zip code, then TLC will return the matching address. It's all very similar to the telephone reverse append process. All we need is a little TLC, and voila! We can identify who purchased that Blue Wool Blazer, size 44 Regular for $200 in the Weehawken store on October 10, 2002. Wasn't that easy?

Maybe. But how do we know this is the correct Claude Johnson? How accurate can we expect this process to be? What if there are two Claude Johnsons in this zip code?

We should keep in mind the fact that TLC obtained the name "Claude Johnson" directly from the credit card. That name and spelling should be very accurate. Otherwise, how can the credit card company make me pay my credit card bill? We don't need to rely on a cashier spelling my name—which in the past has yielded everything from Claud, Clod [my personal favorite], Claude Johnsen, Claude Johsen, or a host of other strange permutations.

Once it has the name Claude Johnson, TLC looks at the zip code provided—in my case, that's 07086. If Claude Johnson is found in that zip code, TLC registers a match, and then returns the address. Respectable, if not responsible, people have assured me that the accuracy rate exceeds 90 percent. Statistically, that's a pretty solid bet.

As it turns out, there is only one Claude Johnson in Weehawken, NJ 07086. There might be a Claude Johnson in zip code 07094 that should be considered. But that zip code is 22 miles away and I don't drive that far to buy a $200 sports coat.

Still, what if there were two Claude Johnsons in zip code 07086? This is where the demographic profiling comes into play. The profiling has defined our store's customer as 40 to 60 years of age. The other Claude Johnson is 21 years old, a punk rocker and has never owned a jacket, let alone a sport coat. Hopefully, this is not my Claude Jr.

If there are 2 Claude Johnsons, TLC can return both names to us, grading each one as to the probability that it's the correct customer. It will be our decision whether to contact one or both of the names. Using some common sense, we would not spend a lot of money communicating to this punk rocker. This leads us to the final test ...

Let's try to **communicate** with a mailing. If our mystery man Claude responds to the mail piece, we can be reasonably sure that we've captured the correct Claude Johnson, age 60, in zip code 07086. With any attempt at identification, we can never be sure that we've made a match. Nevertheless, results speak loud and clear.

One of my clients sent out 162,000 names to a third party data provider for a bit of sleuthing. With the experience that the third party company had gained from Telephone Reverse Append analysis, they were able to develop a scoring algorithm, balancing the accuracy of the information and the value of the customer to the retailer. This scoring placed each of the 162,000 names into 1 of 4 tiers:

	% of Total	Count
Tier 1—Best Customers	35%	57,375
Tier 2—Probably Customers	53%	86,063
Tier 3—Possibly Customers	8%	13,500
Tier 4—"Forget about it!" Customers	3%	5,063
	Total	162,000

In all likelihood, we would not pay much for the bottom two tiers—those "Possibly" or "Forget About It" names and addresses. We're not that desperate to increase our Christmas card list. But wouldn't we like to identify those "Best Customers"? Shouldn't we test the "Probably Customers"? The 2 groups total over 143,000 customers.

With a little **TLC**, we can create over 143,000 additional new customer records. We can **communicate** to 57,375 very valuable (Tier1-Best) customers with a high degree of accuracy. With a slightly lower degree of accuracy, we can test another 86,063 potential customers (Tier2-Probable Customers). If our ultimate test, the mailing, validates our information, then our ability to identify customers at the point of sale has been quadrupled.

Transactions **L**ove **C**ustomers, indeed. Retailers love customers too, or they should. So let's use all the tools we have in order to go out and find out who they are! It's time to show our customers a little **TLC**.

My Suggestion:

Take a look at how advanced modeling and statistical analysis can improve both the quantity of customers we are able to identify, and the quality of information we have about those customers.

TLC is not the only method of identifying the customer at the point of sale, but it should be part of our overall strategy. The challenge is to capture customer's information in order to identify the customer at POS. With a challenge this big, we can leave no stone unturned.

(Wk 4: Simply the BEST)

"Who Is My Customer?"

As we have seen over the last few weeks, it's a good question. Here's an even better one:

"Who Is My Best Customer?"

Have you looked at your best customers recently? Remember the four tiers of customers that we identified last week:

- Tier 1—Best Customers
- Tier 2—Probably Customers
- Tier 3—Possible Customers
- Tier 4—"Forget about it!" Customers

That top tier, normally representing just 10 percent of our total customer base, depending upon the retailer, generates 35–65 percent of our sales. Studies have shown that the top 10 percent of our customers produces 100 percent of our profits. What does this say about the rest of our customers? The truth is: they drain our profits.

A famous bank robber was asked why he kept robbing banks. He said, "That's where the money is, stupid." In the retail industry, the money is in the top ten percent of our customers. So it's worth asking: Do we know who they are?

Let's hope our store managers do. After all, they interact with these people. But do they know their store's Top 25% of customers? What about the top 10%? What about the top 10 customers? *Do they know those customers by sight, and by name and purchase history?*

My Suggestion: (It may take some diplomacy to administer, but here's a pop quiz)

Without offering time for preparation, let's ask our store managers to list their top 25 customers by name.

Then, we'll check their work against our customer database. If we have the guts, we can give the same test to the store associates. The answers that we receive will tell us a great deal about our staff's interaction with the customers.

I've done this exercise several times, and it always surprises everyone when even the "good store managers" can identify only about half of their best customers. (Maybe we should reward the store manager who knows the most Best Customers.) Why is this?

We should start by noting that the store manager doesn't work every hour that the store is open. Obviously, customers will come in when the store manager isn't around to see them. Perhaps one customer went on a shopping spree, while the manager was on vacation. Another customer may be serviced by different people at different times—the store personnel may not be accustomed to merging their client books to find the best customers. Even if the retailer has CRM software for tracking customer purchases, the sales staff may not have access to, or may not be using the information.

Still, it's worth asking: If our store managers don't know who the best customers are, can we really be providing extraordinary service to them? We'd better be. These are the folks that give us *all* of our profits.

Quite literally, we can't do enough for this particular group. If we've done everything we can think of, let's do something more. Our efforts will come back to us tenfold. The highest return on investment in the retail industry is dollars spent on our best customers.

Janet Murphy, President of Ogden Associates, graciously agreed to let me include the following short and sweet "exhortation". That's her word—I don't know any words that big. I hope you heed Janet's advice.

==

You and Your Best Customers: Ships Passing in the Night?

Are you in the dark? Are your most valuable customers anonymously passing in and out of your stores? Let's hope not. But you know that some are. Here are some <u>clues</u> to help you identify whether you're wasting marketing dollars on people who will never buy, while slighting your store's biggest fans, and ignoring the potential customers who are right under your nose.

Clue #1: *Your store managers can't tell you who their best customers are.*

If you don't coddle your best customers, you're likely to lose them. If you don't even know who they are, you've got to catch-up with your competitors, who do know. You need to work actively to retain your best customers, and find others like them.

You can start today. Pull together your in-house information. Rent third-party lists to supplement your company information. Use whatever resources you have available to identify and differentiate your customers, starting with the most valuable ones. Decide how you will make information available to employees throughout the company who must show these customers they're appreciated.

Clue #2: *Your marketing people are sending out the same mailings, e-mails or circulars to all your customers.*

After your best customers leave the store, you should tailor your communication specifically to them. Do you want your longtime customers, who know your stores and love your merchandise, to receive the same communication as the one-time shopper who bought a single item at third markdown?

Your loyal customers like you. You should reciprocate! If they wander, find out why. Your actions should be based on who your best customers are, what they buy, what else they like, how they like to receive information (mail, e-mail, etc.), and how you can serve them better!

Clue #3: *You're not truly innovating to engage customers.*

You won't survive long without innovative strategies. Success today requires much more than simply responding to market demand. Your company may be leaner, more efficient, and more focused on near-term ROI than it was a few years ago. But in the process, please don't eliminate your innovative spirit.

Every day, in a thousand ways, you and everyone in your workplace must consider new and innovative ways to get close to the customer. Create incentives for your employees to encourage new ideas. Reward the best ideas, wherever they originate. With customer focus and innovation, you'll unify and energize your company.

Clue #4: *You're bogged down. You want to bring your company to the next level of CRM, but are daunted by the necessary investments in systems and people.*

Just do it! Start today! Forget the big, expensive, time-consuming projects. Right now, you can make a simple, action-oriented plan, and revise it as you move along. Consider service providers to keep the costs down, before you invest in in-house systems. Use experts to help develop and implement your strategy, targeting where and when you need help. Do the rest in-house. Create near-term targets. Often, the incremental sales you earn can fund longer-range initiatives.

Clue #5: *Your Merchandising people aren't full-fledged members of your CRM team.*

Merchants are the leaders of most retail companies, and their wholehearted involvement in any initiative boosts its priority and momentum. Further, customer relationships start with giving the customers the merchandise they want, when they want it. Without top-level Merchandising commitment to CRM, how can your company talk substantively and persuasively with individual customers?

The Merchandising organization has a vital interest in building loyalty with your best customers. If you don't have a CRM team or steering committee, take action to build one, and include every customer-serving department: merchant, marketing, customer service, store operations, and credit. This group will be responsible for the internal exchange of information about your top customers, and for presenting a unified face on any programs directed to them.

Clue #6: *Your company isn't leveraging your customer base as an important corporate asset.*

With competition always at your heels, strong customer relationships are your most important asset. The competition cannot replicate your unique customer franchise. Your customer information, once collected and analyzed, will reveal opportunities to build more business with the customers who love you.

Go for it! Clean up and enhance your data. Revisit your privacy policies and make sure your data is secure. Good information will unveil the secret of where your marketing and operational dollars are best spent. Confirm your instincts, and leverage your information assets to increase sales and profits, and build shareholder value.

Get moving with your customer strategies, lest you and your best customers seem like ships passing in the night!

Chapter II

February—Cruising Down Loyalty Lane

(Wk 1: Proclivity and propensity)

"What is this thing called loyalty? This crazy thing called ... "

I'm sorry, Cole Porter. It's February, and I couldn't help myself. As we pen our Valentine pledges of undying devotion, it's worth considering that other "L" word. In the grand affair between customer and retailer, what is this thing called "loyalty", anyway? It's not just about our pet dog, Spot. In retail, loyalty is the customer's *propensity* or *proclivity* to repurchase at our store. It is measurable and can be managed to some extent.

You've heard of Jane Austen's *Pride and Prejudice*? How about Claude Johnson's *Proclivity and Propensity*? Get a cup of tea. Sit by the fire. Brace yourself for a life-changing literary tale of love, longing, and, if we're lucky, loyalty.

In the world of retail, the importance of "loyalty, loyalty, loyalty" is second only to "location, location, location." As we discussed last week, our best customers are the ones that drive our business, and more importantly, drive our profits. Loyal customers buy more and are more profitable. Even better, they tell their friends about us, are more forgiving of mistakes, and are more responsive to marketing efforts. Just like good ol' Spot, they're a retailer's best friends.

ADVICE FOR THE LOYALTY-LORN: **Loyalty does not require card carrying membership in a club!** Say that ten times. Tape it to your mirror so that it is the first thing you see in the morning.

This is not to diminish the value of a card-based loyalty program, a subject we'll turn to next week. When choosing between two stores, customers are likely to go where they are members of a loyalty program. A card-based loyalty program, if properly run, can be the tie-breaker. But it's not a panacea. Nor is it the only way to affect *proclivity* and *propensity*. Loyalty is built in any number of ways. Here are some suggestions:

A. **Get The House In Order.**

If we don't have a clean store, with sufficient staff and inventory, the customer is unlikely to return, whether or not we have a loyalty program. Let's get the housekeeping issues off the table, before we invite the guests. No one is that loyal.

B. **Don't Try To Buy It.**

When it comes to loyalty, price is a factor—but not the most important factor. Different things are important to different people.

A store selling the same item at a ten percent discount isn't such a great draw anymore, particularly when a crisp $50 bill barely fills the gas tank. Anybody can reduce price. In most cases, the motivational value of a 10% discount simply disappears when other factors are considered—like being *recognized* upon entering the store. In the end, money can't buy me loyalty.

C. **Don't Buy It. Build It. Remember The Relationship.**

Think of your maitre d' at a favorite restaurant. The most effective hosts (and thus, the most successful restaurants) are those that recognize us when we come in. Restaurant industry studies have revealed that the most important factor in selecting a restaurant is the customer's expectation of being recognized. The best chefs in the world can't do what a "plateful of recognition" can. We go where everyone knows our name.

Nobody can remember every person who has been in their store—except my wife, Tina, who remembers everyone she ever met, including those kids in the playpen next to hers. However, we can and should **remember and recognize** those who buy often and buy a lot.

D. **Be near. They want to be close to you.**

"Location, location, location" is a major motivator. We may have all the other elements to affect *proclivity* and *propensity*, but if we don't have proximity (that other "P" word), then we won't have a loyal customer.

Loyalty is defined as "the *propensity* to re-buy." We may have the best product in the world, but if our store is in Virginia and the customer lives in Idaho, the *propensity* to re-buy is adversely affected. **Do ya think?**

What can we do about that? Do we open a store in Utah? No. Well, maybe we could open one only for the winter ski season. Could we create a store where proximity has no limits? Ah....

We're talking about the Worldwide Web. What better way could there be to reduce the impact that proximity has on the *propensity* to repurchase? Admittedly, other factors, like a relationship with the salesperson and hands-on exposure to the merchandise, still come into play. But we have nullified the proximity issue.

E. **If you love them, let them know.**

There is no loyalty without **communication** to and from the customer. **Communication** at the right time with the right message will increase the customer's *propensity* to return to the store, whether or not there's a formal, card-based program in place.

We can't let memberships or a piece of plastic lull us into complacency. There are plenty of people who "sign up" for our loyalty card, and never show their face in our store again. On average, 50 percent of those customers who signup for a loyalty program never return for a second purchase.

A steady barrage of coupons and catalogues won't do the trick. We need to let our loyal customers know that we've missed them and that we would love to see them come back (and use their discount offer).

At the same time, we need to **communicate** to new people, to increase the probability of a return purchase. We want to thank them for spending time in our store, and express our hope that they will return soon (and take advantage of that special offer we've extended).

My Suggestion:

> **Loyalty is a many splendored thing. Don't put all your eggs in the basket of a card-based loyalty program.**

Learn to do the little things that increase *proclivity* and *propensity*.

(Wk 2: Card-based loyalty)

It shouldn't be hard to guess this week's topic. After all, it's time to celebrate Valentine's Day—the greatest card-based loyalty program ever created.

If we're talking about building loyalty, there is one method that always seems to get the most attention—and not without some justification. The card-based loyalty program can be one of our most-effective methods, both for identifying our customer, and for building that ever-valuable *proclivity* and *propensity*.

Notice I said *"most effective"*. That's not a typo. The card-based loyalty program is *"most effective"* because it helps us identify customers and builds loyalty among only a select portion of our customers: those people that join the program.

If managed properly, a card-based loyalty program might solve most of our problems. However, it won't solve them all. Additional methods must be employed to capture those customers who are not card-carrying members of the club.

Still, if we have no alternative method of identifying our customers, then, at the very least, our card-based program will enable us to identify the customers who bring the choice piece of plastic. Even better, it will give us the ability to track these customers' purchases. Obviously, the larger the percentage of the customer base joining the program, the more effective (albeit costly) our program will be.

On the flip side, if the percentage of the customer base joining the program is too small, we will be forced to rely increasingly on other means of identification. Eventually, the loyalty program will be too expensive, or will become such a small part of the marketing effort that it will die a slow, agonizing death. That's never pretty, for the retailer or the customer.

Am I against card-based loyalty programs? Not at all. But, for some companies, card-based loyalty programs will not work. Indeed, over half of such programs have failed to generate the expected payoff. Nevertheless, for the right company, these programs can be a boon to sales efforts. They can create an opportunity to **communicate** to the customer base that may not be provided by any other database marketing program.

For those brave enough to proceed, what factors should we consider when setting up a card-based loyalty program?

First, we need to create a "joining" process—think of those "get out the vote" campaigns that show up around election time. When customers sign up to participate, they will receive a card, which must be presented at the point of sale. This allows us to track a sale back to a specific customer. To encourage our customers to participate, we will offer an incentive. If customers will sign-up, carry the card (they're not that heavy), and present it at the point of sale, then they will earn some kind of reward. As the Canadians say, not too difficult, eh?

Not too cheap, either. As we learn each Valentine's Day, love and loyalty have their price. Before we launch our loyalty program, we should also consider how much this process might cost us. It's more than a big dinner out and a box of chocolates.

Assuming we have 1 million customers in our loyalty program, we're talking over $2.5 million, in the first year. If your program is planned to be smaller, you can apportion the costs. Then, we should plan on spending over $4 million in the second year. With that money, you could buy my hometown of Boone, North Carolina. I'm not sure what you'd do with it, though. The loyalty program might be a better investment.

Take a look at what this earns us …

How does $25 million in *incremental sales* sound? Would we spend 3.5 million to increase sales over $25 million?

At a keystone gross margin, this would be an additional $12.5 million of gross margin dollars. Of course, this is a best-case scenario. The first retail CFO that I ever worked with said, "Potential sales are like air in a balloon. Pop the balloon and it is gone, never to return."

What if we made a mistake, and were a little slow in generating the expected incremental sales? Would we spend $3.5 million to increase sales by $20 million? Is it worth it for $15 million or $10 million? Most CFO's acknowledge that incremental sales generate two to three times as much profit as base sales. If the sales are truly achievable and incremental, then there is a tremendous upside for a card-based loyalty program.

I'm guessing that the last bit got everyone's attention. I'm also guessing that the CFO still has a couple of concerns:

How can we prove that those incremental sales actually come from the loyalty program?

Glad you asked. This is the major advantage of putting the card in the hands of the customer. In order for the loyalty cardholders to receive the program's rewards, they must identify themselves with the card, at the point of sale. This provides for very detailed tracking and measuring.

But aren't we just rewarding customers who would shop anyway?

This is true. It's also true that we are enhancing customer loyalty through the rewards. Those loyal customers, as a group, will generate incremental sales from the implementation of the loyalty program. Certainly, a portion of the incremental sales planned and measured will come from current customers. Naturally, another portion of the incremental sales will come from new customers who join our loyalty program.

My Suggestion:

> **When it comes to card-based loyalty programs, the key to success is to be clear in your purpose, and realistic in your expectations.**

Remember, this is a "most effective" solution, not a universal cure-all.

The loyalty program will not solve all our problems of customer identification, nor will it transform *proclivity* and *propensity* on its own. But if executed properly, it can have a dramatic impact, both in our ability to identify and track the purchases of our best customers, and to generate incremental sales.

If we don't have a card-based loyalty program, the thought of starting one is worth consideration. If we already have one, it's worth asking: is it yielding the benefits it should?

Take the loyalty oath today:

> **"My best customers produce 100 percent of my profits. I will spend at least 50 percent of my time thinking about what I can do for them!"**

(Wk 3: Cost of doing business)

Is your heart still beating after last week's *Jem?* Have you recovered from the thought of spending a few million dollars to recognize and reward your loyal customers? The CFO still looks a little pale and shaken. But at least his eyes are wide open.

In the example offered last week, we hoped to create a database of 1 million customers, at an expected cost of $2.5 million in the first year, and $4 million in the second year. Of course, the expected return on the investment more than paid for the cost of the program. We estimated an increase in incremental sales of $25 million dollars in the first year. Our decision to proceed was quick and easy.

But it wasn't painless. To no one's surprise, our CFO did have a couple of questions. We'll address the most obvious one this week:

"Where does that cost of $2.5 million dollars go, anyway?"

It's not a bad question. If we're planning to implement a card-based program, we better have a good idea of what lies around the bend. At the very least, we should calculate the expenses, and allocate the money to pay for them. Forewarned is forearmed.

1. **Additional Payroll**

    Nothing gets done by itself. A major undertaking like this will require people to do things they're not doing now. Personnel must be assigned. Job responsibilities may change so significantly that payroll will have to be budgeted as a new expense. Since most employees receive benefits, we will also need to add benefits costs to that increased payroll.

2. **Legal**

    There's always a lawyer lurking somewhere. It's easy to forget, but if we are making a binding commitment to our customers (reward points, etc.), we'd better have an attorney review the wording. The more states in which we have locations, the more time and expense may be required.

3. **Data entry/Data processing**

    Depending upon our current environment, there may be data entry costs for converting data from the customer application (which includes name, address, customer number, and demographic information) into computer records. The expense for this data conversion can run from zero, if the customer self-enters the data at a kiosk or on the web, to more than a $100,000 for 1 million applications.

We should probably budget for some data entry expenses. There's always something that needs to be converted. Some outside data processing might be required for data validation, de-duping, and historical record conversion.

4. **Software/Hardware**

Many companies make the mistake of budgeting the expense of software and hardware and then forget about the rest. "All I really need is the system and the rest will take care of itself," said the CRM manager, as his budget ballooned beneath him. Depending on the starting point, the software/hardware cost can range from a little to a lot. Doesn't everything?

Don't forget the software/hardware issues like:

- the method of entering the customer's name/address information from the application (if not self-entered by the customer).
- the method of capturing the customer number on the sales transactions.
- the transmission of the customer number and the sales transaction to a host computer where the customer database resides.
- the database marketing software that will not only update the customer record with transactions, but register the reward points as if they were a financial commitment, which is exactly what they are. Call it another Accounts Receivable System, if you like.
- the methods for segmenting, selecting, communicating, and measuring results of customer communications.

5. **Beta Test**

Don't jeopardize the loyalty program by trying to implement it without a beta test. Depending upon the retailer, this test can run from 3 months to a year, in select stores. I know one retailer who is still testing for 3 years without rolling the program out. Is he really that afraid to make a decision? Because of the short timeframe for a beta test, it may not offer hard statistics for the long-range effect on customer loyalty—that is something measured over a period longer than a few months. However, it will test the programs, procedures, processes, and training, as well as measure the degree to which the loyalty program is understood and accepted by the customers.

6. Employee Training

Strict monitoring of the beta test will identify aspects of the program that require extra employee training efforts. The development and presentation of that training to numerous locations can be a large expense. But if the store-level staff can't execute, the whole effort goes down the drain.

Not that I've ever seen it, but I'm told that many retailers have "some" turn-over in the stores. The training effort never ends. Train, train, and retrain is the mantra.

7. Enrollment Kits

Now that we've built it, we need to be sure they come. We want to enroll as many people in the program as possible. The enrollment kit consists of an explanation of the loyalty program, the rules of the game, the application, and probably some marketing message from the retailer.

We'll probably need alternate versions of the kit, for different settings: signup table, point of sale, or off-site (a sporting event for example). We'll also want an envelope package for mailing to a prospect or a customer who is not yet a member.

8. Welcome Kits

Once people do sign up, we must welcome them to the program, reinforcing the benefits and giving them a reason to use their card. A package should be sent immediately after the customer record is built in the computer system.

We can send either a Basic Welcome Kit, for a new member joining the program, or an Auto Enrollment Welcome Kit, for any customer already in the database prior to the inception of the loyalty program. Auto enrollment for long-time customers may happen twice—initially during the beta test, and again during the rollout. Even after the rollout, non-member customers will be identified in the customer database and can still be auto-enrolled in the future.

9. Newsletters

This one is optional. If we have some unique information for the members, the newsletter is a great vehicle for communicating it. Otherwise, does anyone really need another newsletter? Are there people whose daily exercise regimen is simply to empty their mailbox?

10. Other

This is also known as a contingency fund. The CFO will love it. The truth is: no one can forecast every expense that might occur over the life of the project. Let's give ourselves some slack. Consulting fees should be included in this category. After all, I have to get budgeted someplace.

11. Points

This is the big enchilada—the most expensive budget item, and the most important as well. Funding for points should run between 3–5 percent of net sales, in order to be viewed as viable in the eyes of our customers. For a $100 million dollar retailer, this cost comes in at $3–5 million dollars. Yikes! Somebody get that CFO a glass of water, fast!

Nevertheless, let me make the following points for points:

1) Most retailers will set a threshold dollar value. Depending upon the size of the threshold, a large or small portion of the points may never be allocated.

2) I don't know a retailer that gets 100% redemption of the points that are issued. This disparity is known as breakage. CFO's often revel in breakage, but it's not always good news. A large breakage factor will point towards a sick loyalty program. Active redemption signifies active participation by the customer.

If we're still feeling up to it, let's take a look at the budget for a $250 million dollar retailer:

Budget Amount	Expense Category
$ 100,000	Additional payroll/benefits
$ 30,000	Legal
$ 62,000	Data entry/Data processing
$ 500,000	Software/Hardware
$ 75,000	Beta test
$ 200,000	Employee training
$ 55,000	Enrollments
$ 155,000	Enrollment kits
$ 200,000	Newsletters
$ 100,000	Other
$1,700,000	Points/Rewards
$3,177,000	Total

These expenses are for the first year. As we've discussed, the second year will be budgeted over $4 million dollars, primarily due to the increase in points awarded. As frightening as this might sound, the list above is not all-inclusive. Of course, the budgets will differ vastly from retailer to retailer. But no matter how we put the numbers together, we are making a sizeable commitment.

My Suggestion:

> **For those implementing a card-based loyalty program, be sure to consider all the hidden expenses.**

Did someone say, "You can't put a price on loyalty?" Let's try.

(Wk 4: HOV lane)

Are we limping along in the Loyalty Lane?

For all the bravado and high hopes that accompany the launching of a loyalty card, too often our interest fades, once the program is in place. Under the illusion that our CRM work is done, we fail to utilize the information generated by the loyalty card. Complacency is the death knell of a loyalty program.

To use a driving analogy: A card-based loyalty program is the HOV lane for retailers. For those who live in a rural area or work at home—the HOV (high-occupancy vehicle) lane allows commuters a faster track to work and home. Likewise, a card-based loyalty program gives us an opportunity to separate ourselves from the pack. It has the potential to provide us the quickest, most effective path to our destination.

But by itself, the HOV lane won't get us there. The road may be laid out in front of us, but it's up to us to hit the gas. The loyalty card is only the means by which we identify the customer and it facilitates our **communications** with our customers. We must make the move. If we rely solely on our card to build customer loyalty, we'll soon find ourselves in the breakdown lane, limping along as our competitors cruise by us.

Let's keep an eye out for the most common signs of trouble along the customer relations highway:

TOO MUCH CRUISE CONTROL: Complacency in customer acquisition.

Employee turnover in the stores requires continuous attention to blips in acquisition. If they're not monitored, even good store personnel will slacken their efforts. The best employees should be given acknowledgement, and the weak links will require corrective action.

One of my most successful clients will not pay quarterly bonuses to those associates with less than the company average performance in customer acquisition. This drastic step came after two years of nudging, cajoling, and threatening the store personnel—all to no avail. Finally, the president said, "This is as important to our company as inventory control. We must have accountability. There is a big financial impact on our business."

Reinforcement of performance standards for the store personnel is one of the most important facets of any retail customer loyalty program. Remember, the stores are where the action is. No one ever met a customer in the marketing office.

RUNNING LOW ON FUEL: Assuming that "the card" or "points" is enough to keep the customer interested.

There is too much competition for this program to work without communication to the customers. Our competitors are communicating to their customers (who are also our customers) on a very regular basis. If we don't stay in touch, we'll lose our grip. One of the best programs I know **communicate**s with customers every month and sometimes several times a month.

Did I hear someone say the customer gets tired of that?

Certainly, each communication has to be relevant and engaging. It cannot always be an offer of 10 percent off all inventory. The use of different messages, different channels, and different mediums will hold the customer's interest.

The key to success is to make our offer relevant to the customer, by taking into account his or her past purchases. After all, why would we spend all the money to put a card in the customer's hands, except to gain intelligence about his or her buying habits? The whole point of the loyalty program is to provide better service, and to allow us to **communicate** more effectively.

Several years ago, I decided to collect all the communications that my wife and I had received from one major department store. In a year, we received 54 postcards, letters and catalogs. We never spent a dime in the store, but we sure felt wanted— with the "thank you" messages, "haven't seen you in awhile" laments, and the seasonal catalogues. Someone is speaking with our customers all the time. So long as our messages are relevant, rather than repetitive, we'd better be in contact.

MISSING THE TURN: Assuming that once we've got the program right, it will stay that way.

As the business environment and the competition changes, our loyalty program must change as well. A few years ago, who would have thought that loyalty programs would be sending rewards statements out via email? Who would have expected to be sending reminders via voice messaging? Our customer is always changing. Our loyalty program has to keep up.

ROAD NARROWS TO ONE LANE: Building a single channel loyalty program.

A single channel loyalty program is not enough—not when our customer buys via multiple channels. Whether the purchase is in store, from a catalogue, or on the Internet, when a customer buys from any channel, he or she should be rewarded from all channels.

In the same way that we run specials in select departments of the store, it is possible for a special opportunity to be offered in one particular retail channel. But if the promotion can be spread across the board, we should do it.

My Suggestion:

Never take a customer's loyalty for granted.

We need to do the little things right—like recognizing the customer, when we see him or her in our store. We need to do the big things right as well. This means keeping our card-based loyalty program relevant and growing.

As in any personal relationship, loyalty is not built in a day. Nor is it sustained without effort. Loyalty requires constant nurturing, a willingness to adapt to change, and a genuine interest in the other party.

It's never easy. It's definitely not cheap. But it is worth it. When it comes to loyalty, we have to be in it for the long run.

Chapter III

March—Identifying "Keepers"

(Wk 1: Gems of *Jems*)

As any farmer will tell you, the first month of planting doesn't yield much fruit. In fact, a good portion of this particular time of year is spent on "fruitless activity". Then POOF! Suddenly, things start to happen. With a little careful cultivation, the crops are abundant once again.

You don't have to be a farm boy like me to get my drift. Not even a houseplant will do anything if it's left unattended in the dark. But given a little water, feeding, and a moment in the sun, that green leafy thing in the corner might show us a flower or two by the end of the month. Spring is in the air, after all.

City folks, have no fear. We're not going to get any actual dirt under our fingernails here. By now, those familiar with my literary style (who knew I was "literary"?) have probably guessed that there is a point to all this and it's not about crop yields.

We're talking relationships here—so anyone who's commitment-phobic should proceed with caution. Just like a flower in the field, our relationships have to be tended, with care and wisdom.

It's not enough to "Communicate, Communicate, Communicate". We have to "Cultivate, Cultivate, Cultivate". We can't give up, if we want our tree to bear fruit. We need to use every channel available to cultivate our customer! What better month could there be to do it?

Here's some down-home advice from Claude's Almanac: All things that grow are not created equal. Don't mix flowers and weeds.

Let's decide which customers are worth nurturing, and put our energy and resources into those.

When I was a lad, I dated plenty of young women. Still, I didn't have the strength or the financial resources to date all of them. When I first met the woman who would become my wife of 38 years (and counting), I told my roommate, "She's a keeper. I'm going to marry this one." In love, as in retail CRM, you need to identify the keepers quickly, and put your time and effort where it will be rewarded.

How do we do this? Do we simply identify who spends the most money? What is the threshold for "most money"? Of course, the boundaries of the top tier will differ for every retailer. Nevertheless, identifying our "keeper customers" is as simple as dividing the proverbial wheat from the chaff.

When it comes to segmenting our customer base into groups, my friend Brian Woolf offers some of the best advice, in his book *"Loyalty Marketing—The Second Act"*. (Why would any self-respecting wolf spell his name with two o's?). In the book, Brian explains the need to identify four segments of customers, which he calls <u>D</u>iamonds, <u>R</u>ubies, <u>O</u>pals, and <u>P</u>earls (**<u>D-R-O-P</u>**).

As the author of a book of *Jems*, you should know that I like his terminology. Plus, the acronym **D-R-O-P** nicely reflects the decrease in revenue, as we move down the four segments. However, you can assign any name you like to the different groups, if you prefer something more fitting to your business. One client, a sports apparel retailer, named his segments, Single, Double, Triple, Homerun.

The key to effective cultivation is distinguishing between good customers and bad customers, and putting our focus on the retention of those customers who mean the most to our business.

Let's start with a report that sorts our customer database in descending dollars, and then cuts the resulting list into tenths. Does a decile report come to mind? Here's an example:

Decile	% of Total Cust	% of Total Sales	Min Spend	Max Spend
1	10.0%	35.1%	$ 404	$ 7,892
2	10.0%	18.8%	$ 272	$ 403
3	10.0%	13.3%	$ 199	$ 271
4	10.0%	9.9%	$ 150	$ 198
5	10.0%	7.5%	$ 114	$ 149
6	10.0%	5.7%	$ 86	$ 113
7	10.0%	4.2%	$ 63	$ 85
8	10.0%	3.0%	$ 43	$ 62
9	10.0%	1.9%	$ 25	$ 42
10	10.0%	0.6%	$ 1	$ 24
Total	100.0%	100.0%		

On the report, we see that the top 10 percent of customers produced 35.1 percent of our sales. These customers spent over $403 in our store. In the same way, anyone in the second 10 percent spent between $272 and $403, and accounted for 18.8 percent of our business. Using a little common sense, which is never all that common, and some convenient rounding-off, we can create the following segments in our customer base:

I must tell you the first time I had one of my programmers produce a decile report, I said "that can't be correct. Our customers are all about the same." I told the programmer to go back and run the program again. He did with the same results, naturally. That was my eye opener to the possibilities for this thing called Customer Database Marketing at the time.

Monetary Segment	Dollar Threshold	% of Total Cust	% of Total Sales
Diamond	$300+	12.8%	40.3%
Ruby	$200-$299	11.7%	18.9%
Opal	$100-$199	25.8%	24.4%
Pearl	$1-$99	49.7%	16.5%
Total		**100.0%**	**100.1%**

Now that we've made this distinction, and have created the catchy monikers as well, we can **communicate** quickly and clearly across all boundaries of the company, to make the entire organization aware of our most valuable customers. Not everyone outside of the marketing department will care about a decile report. However, everyone should care about customers who spend $300 or more and generate almost half of our sales. This is how we get everyone in the organization involved in retail CRM.

One of my clients, Glik Stores, is a good example of this approach. After identifying the monetary segments of their customer base, Glik's Director of Marketing, Kim Hartmann, developed a retention program, and ingeniously titled "Diamonds Are a Retailer's Best Friend". Now, everyone in the company (marketing, stores, and merchants) can **communicate** knowingly about their Diamond customers and their value to the company.

My Suggestion:

> **Start the spring by segmenting your keeper customers and identifying them throughout the organization.**

When it comes to cultivating, the first challenge is putting our efforts in the right place. In a forest, all we can see is the trees. We should be tending an orchard not a forest.

Next, let's roll up our sleeves …

(Wk 2: Cultivate *every* customer?)

I always liked Uncle Bob. I liked my cousin Jesse, too. I never did like my mean 'ole' neighbor, Jethro. Will that help me determine which customers to cultivate? I don't think so. You don't cultivate customers because you like them. You cultivate customers because they like you.

Once we've separated our <u>D</u>iamonds from our <u>P</u>earls, <u>R</u>ubies from <u>O</u>pals, and weeded out the occasional Cubic Zirconium in our customer base, it's time to make some tough-minded decisions. Which customers are worth keeping? Which are not? The customer may always be right. He or she is not always right for us. Does that sound like odd advice from someone in CRM? What company has customers to spare? Shouldn't we try to keep every customer, good, bad or indifferent?

Needless to say, we definitely want to cultivate customers who spend a lot. None of us needs a consultant for that bit of wisdom. We'd also like to retain those who tell others about their positive experiences with us. It's always nice to have friends, especially friends who have other friends. In short, profitable customers are good ones to cultivate. As they grow, they generate … yep, you guessed it: bigger profits.

What about the others—those who don't quite make it into <u>D</u>iamonds and <u>R</u>ubies? In fact, **<u>D-R-O-P</u>** may be exactly what we should do with them. Do we want to retain unprofitable customers, assuming we can identify who they are? Would we spend money to retain them? If you answered yes, I have a lovely piece of oceanfront property in Arizona to sell you.

Maybe we wouldn't kick these unprofitable customers out of bed. We wouldn't bar the door to them during our Christmas sale. Still, would we spend money attempting to retain them?

The answer to the question, "Do I want to cultivate every customer?" is a resounding "NO."

The proverbs abound: pearls before swine, seeds in rocky soil, good money after bad assuming we don't have unlimited resources. We have to put our money where the profits are, and that means taking care of those who take care of us. CRM-savvy retailers would say: "I have only so much money to spend on customer cultivation. I want to spend it where I will get my greatest return." We begin to do that by breaking our customer database into pieces (segments of customers), then tracking the *retention* of each segment.

Hold up. Wait a minute....

What do we mean by "customer retention"? This depends on who you ask. Every retailer has a different definition. Your company will have to define it for themselves. We do know that retention must be measured over time—it could be year to year, season to season, or quarter to quarter. The determining factor is the number of times we expect our customer to repurchase during that timeframe.

Claude's Preferred Definition of "Customer Retention Rate":

The Customer Retention Rate is the percentage of customers who make 2 or more purchases within 6 months.

Once we segment our customer base, and begin tracking the purchases of each segment, we will soon discover that different segments have different retention rates. More importantly, the various segments will require different efforts and expenditures to 1) maintain their retention rates or 2) increase their retention rates.

Most importantly of all, if we want to increase retention (that's called cultivation, and it's a good thing), we better identify which segments will give us the highest return on our investment of time and money.

Spring, 2002 Purchases						
	***	Total Cust	% of Total Cust	Sales	% of Total Sales	Avg Spend
Tier 1		26,900	8.5%	$ 40,000,000	40.0%	$ 1,487
Tier 2	3.1	60,700	19.1%	$ 29,000,000	29.0%	$ 478
Tier 3	7.1	110,000	34.6%	$ 23,000,000	23.0%	$ 209
Tier 4	22.3	120,000	37.8%	$ 8,000,000	8.0%	$ 67
Total		**317,600**	**100.0%**	**$ 100,000,000**	**100.0%**	**$ 315**

*** Tier 1 premium due to average purchase amount

The chart above reflects retention rates for 4 segments of customers:

Tier 1 = Best

Tier 2 = Better

Tier 3 = Good

Tier 4 = OK

All are previously active customers; none are new. They are tiered according to their value to the company, based on their spring seasonal purchases. The top segment averaged $1,487 for the spring season, which means that the top 8.5 percent of the customers produced 40 percent of the sales. Notice that the bottom tier averaged only $67 for spring. The bottom 37.8 percent of the customers produced only 8 percent of the sales. Clearly, there are customers, and then **there are customers!**

If you don't believe me, take a look at the second column above. It reflects the relative value of the Tier 1 customer to the other tier customers. The Tier 1 customer spends:

- 3.1 times the amount of the Tier 2 customer

- 7.1 times the amount of the Tier 3 customer

- 22.3 times the amount of the Tier 4 customer

For every dollar spent on retention efforts for the Tier 4 customer, we would get 22.3 times more sales with the same expenditure on a Tier 1 customer. It's not too hard to decide whom to cultivate in that scenario.

So in the particular retail environment described on the above chart, what is the current retention rate for the different customer segments? We tracked the spring purchasers into fall, and recorded the purchases of those who did return. The results are represented below:

Spring, 2002 Buyers						
***	Total Cust	% of Total Cust	Sales	% of Total Sales	Avg Spend
Tier 1		26,900	8.5%	$ 40,000,000	40.0%	$ 1,487
Tier 2	3.1	60,700	19.1%	$ 29,000,000	29.0%	$ 478
Tier 3	7.1	110,000	34.6%	$ 23,000,000	23.0%	$ 209
Tier 4	22.3	120,000	37.8%	$ 8,000,000	8.0%	$ 67
Total		**317,600**	**100.0%**	**$ 100,000,000**	**100.0%**	**$ 315**

*** Tier 1 premium due to average purchase amount

Repurchased in Fall, 2002					
	Total Cust	Cust % Retain	Sales	Sales % Retain	Avg Spend
Tier 1	22,000	81.8%	$ 32,000,000	80.0%	$ 1,455
Tier 2	50,000	82.4%	$ 20,000,000	69.0%	$ 400
Tier 3	74,000	67.3%	$ 21,000,000	91.3%	$ 284
Tier 4	67,000	55.8%	$ 12,000,000	150.0%	$ 179
Total	**213,000**	**67.1%**	**$ 85,000,000**	**85.0%**	**$ 399**

First, we can see that the total customer retention for all 4 tiers was 67.1%. The dollars spent in the fall season equated to 85% of the total spring purchases. This is a very high retention rate for any retailer. It's evident that there's already been a whole lot of cultivatin' goin' on.

If we look closely, there are some very interesting statistics in this chart. Tier 1 customers are retained at a rate of 81.8 percent, and the dollars they spent in fall account for 80 percent of spring expenditures.

One might say that we are getting all we can out of that group. Not so fast, Sparky! Each of these Tier 1 customers is worth $1,455 for the fall season. If we can get only 1 additional Tier 1 customer to return and repurchase, it's worth $1,455.

It's also worth noticing that the Average Spend for Tier 3 and 4 customers rises significantly fall vs. spring:
Tier 3 goes from $209 in the spring → to $284 in the fall
Tier 4 goes from $67 in the spring → to $179 in the fall.
Those customers that do repurchase, especially those in the lower tiers, usually spend more than the average customer in their segment.

In the end, the most important thing in this analysis is not the results, but the record-keeping. By measuring customer retention on an ongoing basis, we can see if our cultivation initiatives are working. By segmenting the customer base, we can put our money into retention programs aimed at the most valuable segments and measure to see if they are working.

Finally, by tracking purchases, we can measure the return on our investment in cultivating our valued customers. It may not look like much, but small increases in retention in the top 2 tiers create big increases in incremental sales for the following season. These sales would otherwise have been lost to attrition.

Clearly, when it comes to ROI, it only pays to cultivate the cream of our crop. The top 2 tiers of customers are rewarding our efforts. The bottom tiers are draining our resources.

My Suggestion:

> **If you're going to make the effort to retain customers, then you need the capability to measure your results.**

You must segment the customer base, identify your "keepers", and invest your money and effort in cultivating customers that give you the most bang for your buck. Cultivation is all a matter of care and feeding. The good customers will pay us back ten-fold. The unprofitable customers can eat us out of house and home. It's our job to know the difference.

(Wk 3: Return on investment)

Retailers spend a lot to attract shoppers to their stores. We're not just talking about advertising and promotion, but all costs of doing business at store level: payroll, training, IT, rent. When it comes to planting our fields, we're an ambitious and optimistic group. But too often, when it comes to cultivation, our attention and financial investment run out too early. We plant, but we forget to grow.

Once shoppers make a purchase, what dollars should we spend to increase future business with them? More importantly, which customers should we target, and how can we do it more effectively?

One of my clients gave me a chance to dig into this issue with a recent analysis of the company's yearly mail campaign. This campaign is directed to all active customers, who had purchased in the last 12 months. All customers received the same mail piece.

However, as we discussed last week, all customers are not the same. So this year, we segmented the recipients by month of last purchase, and re-examined the response rate based on the recency of purchase. The results were dramatic—with a clear message about the process of cultivation:

Sooner is always better.

Month of Last Purchase	Total Cust	$.40 ea Cost of Mailing	Resp Rate	# of Resp	Sales	Margin Keystone	ROI
1 Mon Ago	20,000	$8,000	12%	2,400	$240,000	$120,000	1500%
2 Mons Ago	20,000	$8,000	11%	2,200	$220,000	$110,000	1375%
3 Mons Ago	20,000	$8,000	10%	2,000	$200,000	$100,000	1250%
4 Mons Ago	20,000	$8,000	9%	1,800	$180,000	$90,000	1125%
5 Months	20,000	$8,000	8%	1,600	$160,000	$80,000	1000%
6 Months	20,000	$8,000	7%	1,400	$140,000	$70,000	875%
7 Months	20,000	$8,000	6%	1,200	$120,000	$60,000	750%
8 Months	20,000	$8,000	5%	1,000	$100,000	$50,000	625%
9 Months	20,000	$8,000	4%	800	$80,000	$40,000	500%
10 Months	20,000	$8,000	3%	600	$60,000	$30,000	375%
11 Months	20,000	$8,000	2%	400	$40,000	$20,000	250%
12 Months	20,000	$8,000	1%	200	$20,000	$10,000	125%
Total	240,000	$96,000	7%	15,600	$1,440,000	$720,000	750%

NOTE: the Control File responded at 3%

The highest response rate was from the most profitable group of customers for the mailing: recent purchasers. In fact, the group of customers who purchased 1 Month Ago yielded 12 times the return of those customers who purchased 12 Months Ago. The group of customers, whose last purchase was more than 10 months ago, did not generate enough incremental sales even to recover mailing costs.

Looking at the chart, if we could magically replace the 20,000 customers from the oldest group (12 Months Since Last Purchase) with 20,000 recent shoppers, our sales would increase $220,000 and ROI would soar by 1,375 percent. Sign us up for that, right? Where do we find more of those recent customers, who respond at the 12% rate?

They're already there. Like flower bulbs hidden under the dirt, they are buried in the extraordinary delays in our mailing process. All we need to increase our response rate is more frequent mailings, and a streamlined mail process as expressed below. If we can magically cut 30 days out of the time between the transaction and the delivery of the message, we have magically discovered those 20,000 customers will give us 12% response rate.

Consider the typical, time-honored, and time-consuming process for transforming that mail piece from a gleam in the marketing guru's eye into a postcard in the mailbox of our customer:

- We have to pull the mail file of customer records: 2–3 days at best.

- We have to print the piece, which could take anywhere from 3 days to 4 weeks (slack is built in "just in case").

- We have to get it in the mail, which includes presorting the file, laser printing the mailing address, bagging, and delivering the envelopes to the post office. Figure in another 3–7 days (slack is built in "just in case").

- Then it all comes down to the intrepid US Mail. Journeying as they do through rain, snow, sleet and hail, they will try to deliver it in 5–9 business days. Or maybe sometime next year. You never know.

It's not called snail mail for nothing. This process is so inefficient that it's robbing us of our most profitable marketing returns. It gets even worse. Another major time lag can occur when direct mail events are triggered by purchases.

For example, one of my clients sends thank-you letters to key customers for their major purchases. This thank-you goes out the first week of each month, for any major purchases made in the previous month. I'm never one to fault someone for saying thank you. But remember what we've learned: **sooner is always better.**

For the person whose major purchase was made the day after last month's list was pulled, another 30 days will be added from the date of purchase to the day the thank-you letter shows up in the mail. By the time the mail piece arrives, the impact is lost on the customer, who has probably forgotten the whole transaction. For us seniors, it's hard to remember yesterday's transaction.

Given what we've learned about the effects of recency on response rate, how much better would it be if this mailing was done every week, rather than once a month? With a "monthly list pull," the average mail time from the customer's transaction is 15 days (the mid-point between 1 and 30 days). That time could be cut to 3.5 days with a weekly pull. When it comes to cultivation, the early bird gets the worm.

My Suggestion:

> **Put your money and effort into the customers who are most likely to respond to your efforts: the recent purchasers.**

We can do that by streamlining our mailing process.

One Midwest retailer had all the challenges we've discussed, from list pull to printing, to mail services to third class mailing. Initially, the company insisted that the lag time to the customer could not be improved. But with a little work, we were able to pull the list every Monday, to have the mail piece in the customer's hands by Thursday or Friday—just in time for weekend selling.

The goal is to exchange that 1 percent response group with a 12 percent response group. Such a deal! Let's put our money, our marketing and our mailing where it matters. And do it fast!

(Wk 4: *March Madness*)

March Madness is happening this month. What better time to consider that most magical of basketball shots: the long-distance 3-pointer? If we tune in the television, we'll see them popping in all over the place.

When was the last time you had a retail 3-pointer?

When it comes to cultivating the customer, our playbook is pretty limited. For a targeted, direct mail promotion, there are really only **3 Channels of Communication** to the customer:

(1) Mail the customer

(2) Phone the customer

(3) Email the customer

I suppose we could also drive to the customer's home and announce our offer with a megaphone. The neighbors would not be the only ones to call a foul.

The conventional game plan says that we must pick one of these three channels, based on the following factors:

- Length of time to execute
- Cost
- Expected Response rate
- Expected Return on Investment
- Availability of information (mailing address, phone number, email address)

Let's imagine that we are doing a four-week event, targeting 100,000 customers. Keep in mind that a store promotion is not like March Madness, where interest levels peak at the end. As we can see on the chart below, any retail event will show a diminishing response rate over four weeks. Retailers have always wondered about how to sustain a 4-week direct mail event. As the chart below reflects, the response rate goes down over the life of the event.

Total Quantity Mailed, 100,000 Postcards

	# of Resp	Response Rate
Week 1	4,500	4.5%
Week 2	3,200	3.2%
Week 3	1,800	1.8%
Week 4	1,000	1.0%
Total	10,500	10.5%

Here are our three options for contacting our customer:

- **Email the customer**

  Even though email costs the least, it is not normally a stand-alone medium of communication for a very long retail marketing event. With email, the response rate is the smallest of the three channels, and the window for response is only a few days.

- **Phone the customer**

  It's reasonable to expect sales people to call their best customers. It's not reasonable to expect the sales staff to call 100,000 customers in a week, while sales activity continues in the stores.

  Voice messaging is one alternative to having store associates call their customers, but it has drawbacks as well. Like emailing, it costs a fraction of a mail piece, but is not a stand-alone medium for campaigning to 100,000 customers over four weeks. Although the response rates for voice messaging are higher than for email, they are still lower than with a postcard. Again, the window for response is only a few days.

- **Mail the customer**

  This one costs the most, but generates the highest overall response rate and total sales. It also has the longest response rate of the three options, though it too will diminish over a four-week period. Like a fourth-quarter rally, some retailers do see a spike in the response rate in the last days of an offer, as customers rush to take advantage before the clock runs out.

We could choose to play this game in the most predictable way. We could simply pick the most appropriate channel for our event and our budget, and then try to score communication points with the customer through that single method.

My Suggestion:

> **What if you opted to use all three channels of communication? You could try a three-pointer!**

Can't you hear your colleagues cheering wildly on the sideline?

As in any basketball game, part of the challenge is shot selection. We can't fire away at random. The key to the retail 3-pointer is timing. When it comes to cultivating customers for our four-week event, we have to take our best shot at the right moment. Here's the strategy:

1. **We start the game with a direct mail piece.** We mail it and begin tracking results like any good coach.

2. **In the second week, when the team's offense is stuck in a rut and the response rate is tailing off, it's time to execute the old "voice-message play."** This will pump up the team without the use of steroids. Let's check the scoreboard stats:

	# of Resp	Response Rate	Accum
Postcard Only			
Week 1	4,500	4.5%	4.5%
Week 2	3,200	3.2%	7.7%
Week 3	1,800	1.8%	9.5%
Week 4	1,000	1.0%	10.5%
Total	10,500	10.5%	

Pull the trigger on a 2-Pointer

Week 1	4,500	4.5%	4.5%	
Week 2	4,800	4.8%	9.3%	Calls Made
Week 3	1,900	1.9%	11.2%	
Week 4	1,000	1.0%	12.2%	
Total	12,200	10.5%		

1,700 Incremental Responses over Postcard Only

3. At the end of the third week, when the team is dragging (and response rate tails off again), we'll execute a behind-the-back pass with email messaging.

	# of Resp	Response Rate	Accum
Postcard Only			
Week 1	4,500	4.5%	4.5%
Week 2	3,200	3.2%	7.7%
Week 3	1,800	1.8%	9.5%
Week 4	1,000	1.0%	10.5%
Total	10,500	10.5%	

Pull the trigger on a 2-Pointer

Week 1	4,500	4.5%	4.5%	
Week 2	4,800	4.8%	9.3%	←Calls Made
Week 3	1,900	1.9%	11.2%	
Week 4	1,000	1.0%	12.2%	
Total	12,200	12.2%		

1,700 Incremental Responses over Postcard Only

Pull the trigger on a 3-Pointer

Week 1	4,500	4.5%	4.5%
Week 2	4,800	4.8%	9.3% ←Calls Made
Week 3	2,900	2.9%	12.2% ←Emails Sent
Week 4	1,100	1.1%	13.3%
Total	**13,300**	**13.3%**	

<u>**2,800 Incremental Responses over Postcard Only**</u>

… and the buzzer sounds! How did we do?

When the event is over and the points are recorded, we will see that the response rate is the largest it could possibly be. Our three-pointer generated 2,800 incremental transactions. If our average transaction is $50, we have generated $140,000 for a cost of less than $10,000.

Looks like that 3-pointer at the buzzer just won the game. **YEA, YEA, YEA!**

Did someone mention Coach of the Year?

(Wk 5: Customer retention)

Having devoted this month to the effective cultivation of our customers, we've already learned the value of fast action, and the need for eliminating delays in our customer communication. Let's wind up with a quick look at the big picture, and discover why the cultivation process pays off so handsomely. It's all about keeping 'em coming back for more.

A few months ago, I presented the results of a customer analysis to the president of one of my clients. I asked him what his stores' customer retention rate was. His first response was to demand a definition, since that term means many things to many people. Here was my quick comeback:

If 1,000 customers purchased at our store this month, how many will purchase again in the next 6 months? How many will still be our customers in 6 months?

Having thus defined the question, I turned back to the president. He thought for a few seconds. Finally, he proudly announced that 90 percent of his customers would repurchase in the next 6 months. Wow. I was a little shocked. I responded that while he may be right, my experience led me to believe that he might be overestimating his results. I was being unusually diplomatic. If he were right, his retention rate would have been the highest in all of my experience in retail.

In fact, his company's actual retention rate was about 30 percent, leaving him a little room for improvement. Isn't it amazing how removed some executives are from what is really happening in their stores?

This is not a small matter. It's a matter of profitability. Most experts believe that a retailer can increase profits as much as 75 percent by increasing retention as little as 5 percent. The cost of acquiring a customer is 10 or more times the cost to retain a current customer. When it comes to retention, ignorance is definitely not bliss.

We can't bury our heads in the sand. Instead, let's ask ourselves: What is our current retention rate? What percentage of our customers will purchase again within six months?

As usual, the analysis can only be accomplished with a customer database that tracks customer purchases. Using that database, the chart below tracks how long it took to make a second purchase, from a sample of 100,000 customers who had purchased in the month prior to the test.

The number of customers by month of second purchase is

1 month after purchasing	19,000 or 19%
2 months after purchasing	7,000 or 7% second purchasers
3 months after purchasing	4,000 or 4% second purchasers
4 months after purchasing	3,000 or 3% second purchasers
5 months after purchasing	3,000 or 3% second purchasers
6 months after purchasing	2,000 or 2% second purchasers
	Total of 38% for 1st 6 months

In this particular case, the retention rate is 38% over 6 months. But as Noah might have said, the real news is in the arc.

Notice how dramatically the rate falls after the second month. Every retailer will have a different Repurchase Rate Curve—it will vary across seasons, and even geographical area. Still, the general shape will remain the same. Any curve I've seen shows a dramatic falloff from month 1 to month 3, leveling after month 3 or 4, and settling into a rate of 1–3 percent thereafter.

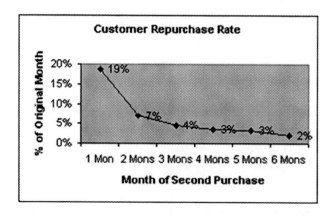

It looks like we've come right back to the whole matter of proper timing. When it comes to cultivating our customers, time is money—the longer we wait to do it, the more we lose. These charts suggest that we have only a short period of time to affect the repurchase rate of our customers. After 60 to 90 days, the probability of our customers returning diminishes to the point that it may not be cost effective to market to them.

My military tactical officer at West Point in the 60's would say, "Knowledge without action costs lives." Thankfully, our stakes are a little lower. Still, we can't afford paralysis by analysis. We can either say, "Woe is me", or make some changes to lift this curve. Keep in mind that a small improvement in the curve equates to a very big increase in sales.

We should:

- **Communicate** to our customers more often and in a more timely fashion, especially after purchases.
- Prevent customers from aging beyond month 3 without having made a purchase.
- Reward loyalty. This will increase transaction counts over time.
- Develop multiple offer programs to stimulate store traffic.
- Consistently measure retention to identify progress in different customer segments.

After my dear, gentle wife saw the curves (in the chart, not my waist), she said, "Strike while the iron is hot." She finally understands what I do all day long.

My Suggestion:

> **You can't start to improve your retention rate until you know where you are right now. Create a chart like the one in this example for your own company.**

With this kind of chart in hand, we're no longer like the clueless CEO, convinced that he's effectively cultivating 90 percent of his customers. We can see our retention rate, in all its glory or shame. We can learn how much time should elapse before we pull the trigger on targeted communications to retain the customer.

We can even go further, and begin to look at a segmented analysis:

How would the curves differ if we included only first time customers? What would it look like for only top-tier customers? Beyond weather, what other factors might explain different regional retention rates? Best of all, we can measure the effectiveness of any retention programs we've put in place.

They say that March comes in like a lion, and goes out like a lamb. Too often, our customers do something similar—roaring in dramatically for that first purchase, only to wander meekly off our radar screen a few months later. Leave them alone and they will not likely come home.

Cultivation is the key. Find your "keeper" customers. Sooner is always better. Use all channels of communication. Pay attention to retention. It will come back to you in profits!

Chapter IV

April—"Where, oh where has my customer gone?"

(Wk 1: Location, location, location)

Okay. It's no secret. We all know the three-word secret to retail success:

Location, Location, Location.

Back when I was a retailer, I thought that old maxim referred to the location of the store. As I get older and wiser (and my wife assures me that I'm at least half-way there), I've realized that there's more to success than that.

It's not only the location of the store that matters. It's the location of the customer that counts. Here's an appropriate question for a retailer on a rainy Monday in April:

"Where Is My Customer?"

Who hasn't wondered that? Let's start by redefining the question. What we really need to know is where our customer *lives*. Remember, proximity to the store is a major part of customer loyalty.

If we know our customer's address, city, state, and zip code, then we have a gold-mine of information. Being able to communicate to them via mail is only one of the advantages. We also have a significant advantage over most of our competitors. If you're one of the few who are already concerned where your customers live, "Pop your chest up soldier. Be proud"!

Those who have not yet tracked their customers' whereabouts had best get on the trail. After all, we can't target them if we don't know where they are. Before we start shooting, let's aim. Where is our customer, anyway?

The easy answer is: nearby. More often than not, our customer is comfortably ensconced in what is called the Store Trade Area, or Store Market Area—also affectionately known as "a place where we have a lot of customers."

For any retailer, the definition of the Store Trade Area is purely arbitrary. But it's essential that our company define it clearly, so that the whole organization is on the same page. Here's a definition I like:

<u>Store Trade Area</u>: **the geography around a store that includes approximately 80 percent of the customers who have purchased.**

You might think I'm fudging, by setting the definition at "approximately 80 percent." Wait until *you* try this. No geography breaks exactly at 80 percent.

Within this definition, there are two subsets:

<u>Primary Trade Area</u>: **The geography that makes up about 50 percent of the store's customer base.**

<u>Secondary Trade Area</u>: **the geography that makes up the balance of 50–80 percent.**

Not too surprisingly, any geography outside the Store Trade Area is defined as Non-Trade Area. Have you ever seen the New Yorker's "A New Yorker's Map of the World"? That unidentified area beyond the Hudson or East River is what we might call the Non-Trade Area for Manhattan.

Attentive and forward-thinking retailers that we are, we have amassed millions of customer and sales records. How can we present and utilize the data to obtain the best intelligence. As we've probably already noticed, having the information and using it effectively are two entirely different things. One of the most obvious and most effective ways we can organize our information is by location. In the following, you will see the data for a representative store in a retail chain.

Assuming we have a customer database that provides the address of each customer and a listing of the customer's sales transactions, we can create a report showing the customer count and sales segregated by zip code. If you calculate the % of total customers and dollars for each zip code, you can sort in descending % of customers and your best zip codes will sort to the top.

Zip Code	Cust Count	% of Total	Accum
10024	1,458	24.1%	24.1%
10025	677	11.2%	35.3%
10023	354	5.9%	41.2%
10021	143	2.4%	43.6%
10028	122	2.0%	45.6%
10128	119	2.0%	47.6%
-----	---	---	---
-----	---	---	---

You very simply can keep going down this report until you get tired or you get to some arbitrary Accum %, say 50%. This will give you the list of zip codes that make up 50% of your customer base and is arbitrarily defined as your **Primary Trade Area** around this store. If you continue down the listing until you get to 80% Accum, you will have added the **Secondary Trade Area** (51–80%) and the rest of the zip codes and the rest of the world are designated as Non-Trade Area for this store.

But do we care? Does it matter where our customer lives?

It only matters if we're trying to find them or **communicate** to them. When we target direct mail pieces, the customers who live in the Primary Trade Area will almost always respond at a higher rate than the customers in the Secondary Trade Area. Similarly, those customers in the Secondary Trade Area will almost always respond at a higher rate than customers in the Non-Trade Area. Why is that? Here are three good reasons:

Location, Location, Location.

I have discovered that proximity to the store is the second most important indicator of a customer's probability of responding to a direct mail piece.

By the way, proximity can be defined by driving distance, subway stops, miles as the crow flies, or whatever criteria suits the region of the country in which we find ourselves.

My Suggestion:

> **Use your wealth of data to identify your Primary and Secondary Trade Areas, and target your marketing accordingly.**

If we're going fishing, it helps to know where the fish are, especially the big ones. Let's find out where our customers are, and then hit 'em where they live.

(Wk 2: Concentration and penetration)

The customers still haven't shown up, eh?

Don't despair. If we can figure out where our customers live, then we don't have to wait for them to show up at our door. We can go out and get them. It's a matter of narrowing down the terrain, and picking the best spots, before we start the hunt. This week's buzzwords are:

Concentration & Penetration

We've already begun to draw the lines that define our store's turf. We know that our Primary Trade Area is that geographical area that encompasses approximately 50 percent of our store's customer base. The Secondary Trade area is the balance remaining, which encompasses up to 80 percent of our customer base. Any geography outside of that is the marketer's no-go zone, otherwise known as the Non-Trade Area. These customers may shop once in a while but as a rule, it is not cost effective to market to them.

With a database to provide our customers' home addresses and purchases, we can produce a Zip Code Concentration report. This allows us to analyze customer concentration; i.e., customer counts by zip code in descending sequence, and to identify those zip codes that make up the vast majority of our customer base.

Detroit Store - Primary Trade Area							
		Customer Distribution			Sales Distribution		
Rank	Zip	Cust Count	% of Total	Accum	Purchases	% of Total	Accum
1	48322	2,335	11.7%	11.7%	$ 951,573	13.4%	13.4%
2	48323	1,274	6.4%	18.1%	$ 581,969	8.2%	21.6%
3	48331	1,092	5.5%	23.6%	$ 390,884	5.5%	27.1%
4	48334	871	4.4%	27.9%	$ 311,762	4.4%	31.5%
5	48034	759	3.8%	31.7%	$ 238,806	3.4%	34.9%
6	48302	504	2.5%	34.2%	$ 239,115	3.4%	38.2%
7	48324	492	2.5%	36.7%	$ 181,368	2.6%	40.8%
8	48076	491	2.5%	39.2%	$ 178,334	2.5%	43.3%
9	48301	426	2.1%	41.3%	$ 156,566	2.2%	45.5%
10	48075	390	2.0%	43.3%	$ 149,887	2.1%	47.6%
11	48336	325	1.6%	44.9%	$ 82,014	1.2%	48.8%
12	48237	317	1.6%	46.5%	$ 82,567	1.2%	49.9%
13	48221	317	1.6%	48.1%	$ 99,674	1.4%	51.3%
14	48025	298	1.5%	49.6%	$ 114,990	1.6%	52.9%
15	48235	298	1.5%	51.1%	$ 113,334	1.6%	54.5%
Trade Area->		10,189	51.1%		$ 3,872,843	54.5%	

Total Store	19,961	$ 7,089,092

Voila! Here are our customers! We can see that a very small number of zip codes make up a very large portion of our customer base and sales for this store. You will also note the ranking of the zip codes. Zip code 48322 is the most important zip code for this store. As I predicted, those people who mean the most to us have been right under our noses all the time.

I've never seen a Zip Code Concentration report in which the store location was not the top zip code. Every retailer seems to know to put the store in the middle of the area where the store has the most customers. Perhaps it just works out that way. Suffice to say, if we're looking for our customer, the first place to start would be very close to home.

Armed with this information, it's not difficult to predict where our next customer can be found. Using the chart, there is a 51 percent probability that our next customer will come from one of those same 15 zip codes. There's an 11.7 percent probability that he or she will come from zip code 48322. If you're a betting man, and what retailer isn't, these are your odds. Take a drive around your zip code. All things being equal, those people you see are probably your customer.

Of course, all things are not equal. As terrific as the Zip Code Concentration report is, it does have one flaw. It does not allow for the fact that zip codes have different quantities of people from which to draw. We don't merely need to know in which areas most of our customers are concentrated. We need to know how effectively we've penetrated each zip code. For this, we need a little help from our friends and a little more number crunching as well.

Using a third party data source, we need to gain access to a new number: the number of households in each of the zip codes that make up our Primary Trade Area. From there, we can produce a Zip Code Penetration report similar to the one below.

	Zipcode Penetration Report					
	Concentration		Penetration			
	Cust	% of	HH		Ranking	
Zip	Count	Store	Count	Pene	Conc.	Pene
48322	2,335	11.70%	12,012	19.40%	1	1
48323	1,274	6.40%	6,807	18.70%	2	2
48331	1,092	5.50%	8,661	12.60%	3	3
48334	871	4.40%	7,928	11.00%	4	4
48302	504	2.50%	6,540	7.70%	6	5
48324	492	2.50%	6,567	7.50%	7	6
48301	426	2.10%	5,785	7.40%	9	7
48025	**298**	**1.50%**	**6,082**	**4.90%**	**14**	**8*****
48034	**636**	**3.80%**	**16,268**	**3.91%**	**5**	**9*****
48076	491	2.50%	10,899	4.50%	8	10
48075	390	2.00%	9,728	4.00%	10	11
48336	325	1.60%	11,671	2.80%	11	12
48237	317	1.60%	12,818	2.50%	12	13
48221	317	1.60%	17,233	1.80%	13	14
48235	298	1.50%	20,557	1.40%	15	15

As you might guess, the penetration column is calculated simply by dividing the number of customers in the zip code by the number of households in the zip code. Don't worry—it's okay to try this at home. Overall, the general ranking (to the right) is similar to the Zip code Concentration report. The most notable differences are in zip codes 48025 and 48034.

We should keep in mind: the information we generate in this endeavor is only as good as the data we put in. Just as all zip codes are not created equal, neither are all Third Party Providers. It seems very easy for someone to have counted the number of homes on the street. Have we accounted for multi-family dwellings? Empty homes? New homes built since the last survey? When was this information last updated, anyway?

Don't assume that third party data is correct. Be wary of the gift-bearer. Test one source against another. If the source will not allow a test, then get another source. There are plenty of them out there, and many of them acquire their data from the same original source.

If our information is correct, the Concentration and Penetration reports should lead us very close to the object of our desire: our occasionally elusive customer. Even better, we know there are more customers where he or she came from.

My Suggestion:

Target your marketing efforts in the areas where our customers live.

You not only will reach your loyal customers, you'll find new customers. Using the Concentration and Penetration reports, the odds are in our favor. If we dig in the right spot, we've got a very good chance at finding the buried treasure.

(Wk 3: Trade area defined)

Now that we've found our customer, and we know where he or she lives, it's not too hard to guess what comes next. If we've identified our Primary and Secondary Trade Area, let's use this information to go get some more customers like the ones we have. Enough number crunching, right? Let's start mailing!

Using our Zip Code Penetration report, we can rent the names and addresses of all the non-customers in our Primary Trade Area. Then, we can send them a special offer to stop by the store. After all, we know that we'll be mailing to the people who have the highest probability to become customers. All we have to do is **communicate**, and prepare for the stampede of eager new patrons!

Imagine that we mail 150,000 pieces, at a total cost of about $100,000, including creative, printing, mail services, postage and the cost of the list. We can assume a 1 percent response rate, which is fairly common on prospect mailings. If our average transaction is $50, and our margin is keystone, we have generated $75,000 in sales. Congratulations.

There's only one problem:

We just lost $62, 500! [$100,000 - $75,000x50% margin = $62,500 in the red] Oops. Sorry, boss. It all looked so good on paper. What did we do wrong?

We just did too much of a good thing. To mail 150,000 customers is the equivalent of killing a fly with an elephant gun. Better to opt for a little more analysis, and a little less action. It's not simply a matter of identifying to whom we want to mail. It's more important to identify to whom we do NOT want to mail.

Let's look at a different example:

This time, we'll start by picking one zip code in this store's primary trade area; this zip code has the third highest penetration level on the store's report. As you can see, the zip code has 16,268 households, which is quite large.

> **Zip code 48221**
>
> 16,268 Households
>
> 636 Customers
>
> 3.91% Customer Penetration Rate

$51,953 Average Household Income

3.7 Distance to the store (Miles)

By now, we have surmised that mailing to all 16,268 households in the zip code is not a very smart thing to do. We need to narrow the field. If we can work with a smaller geography than zip code, using the same information about the people in the household, it will be much easier for us to exclude the households unlikely to respond.

Where does one find geography smaller than a zip code? What are our alternatives?

1. **Zip +4**

   This is the post office's attempt to address mail at a level below zip code. It's a good idea for the post office, but not something that will be universally used in direct marketing any time soon.

2. **Block Group**

   Frankly, this is something that I just don't understand. Even if I did, I probably couldn't explain it. It's all too much for a simple Southern boy.

3. **Census Tract**

   This means something to the census bureau, but nothing to us humans.

4. **Carrier Route.**

   Now this one I like. The carrier route encompasses the geography for which a mail carrier can deliver mail in an 8-hour day. I like this alternative because:

   (a) it's consistent with our understanding and use of zip code information,

   (b) it is relatively stable,

   (c) information is almost universally available down to the Carrier Route level,

   (d) the households in a Carrier Route tend to be very similar demographically because all the delivery points in the carrier route are contiguous, and,

   (e) relatively speaking, it is very inexpensive to acquire information at the Carrier Route level.

Let's go back to our case study and see how this plays out:

Zip code 48221 (43 carrier routes)

Zip Total	Min.	Max.	
3.7	2.4	5.2	Distance to the Store
16,268	260	539	# of Households in the Carrier Route
$51,953	$19,751	$145,092	Average Household Income

From the chart above, several figures pop out at us:

- The post office has determined that it takes 43 mail carriers to deliver the 16,268 households in zip code 48221. Is it any wonder that the cost of stamps keeps going up?
- The distance to the store ranges from 2.4 miles to 5.2 miles. We should remember that proximity to the store is the major factor in response to a direct mail piece.
- The number of households in each Carrier Route ranges from 260 to 539. If we can pick the best carrier routes, that's a lot better than working with 16,258 total households for the entire zip code.
- The average household income ranges from $19,751 to $145,092. Do we really think the $20,000 household has the same buying pattern as the $145,000 household? We need to target the income strata that matches our customer.

Now we can run our penetration report again, but this time using our new geography: the Carrier Route.

Zip code 48221 (43 carrier routes)

CR	HH	Cust	Pene%
C016	366	30	8.20%
C014	344	26	7.56%
C022	281	19	6.76%
C029	320	21	6.56%
C026	405	25	6.17%

---	---	---	---
---	---	---	---
C033	437	7	1.60%
C004	424	6	1.42%
C017	374	3	0.80%
C012	386	3	0.78%
Total	16,268	636	3.91%

From the chart above, we can see that the Carrier Route Penetration ranges from 8.20% down to .78%. We could take the time to ask why our penetration rates are so low on those bottom Carrier Routes. Or we could simply thank our lucky stars that we have this information, and exclude those routes from our mailing.

The smart strategy is to select the Carrier Routes with a penetration of 4.0% and above. This would have us mailing the top 6,647 potential customers. We'll certainly be spending less money than if we mailed to an entire zip code. Moreover, our response rate is likely to increase. By using the Carrier Route to target the marketing effort, one of my clients just received a 3.17% response rate, significantly larger than the earlier 1% response.

Too many retailers approach a mailing with too much money and too little information. Boxes of expensive mail pieces are sent blindly to anyone in a zip code who's not already a customer—all in the hopes that enough people will respond to make the mailing profitable.

Most of the time, it doesn't work. The vast majority of prospect mailers do not result in an immediate return on investment. All that's left is the hope that the few people who did respond will eventually make the whole enterprise profitable with their continued, lifetime purchases. [A lifetime is a long time to wait to see if the prospecting worked.] Sometimes, even this is a pipe dream.

Prospecting for new customers is not unlike prospecting for oil. It's not enough to know where to drill in general. In order to make a profit, we need to know the EXACT spot.

My Suggestion:

Once you think you've found your customer, you should think again.

You need to narrow it down from zip code Concentration to zip code Penetration. Then, go one step further, and break it down by Carrier Route. It's not enough to know where our customer is. We have to figure out where they are not.

(Wk 4: Radiation: the *good,* the *bad* & the *ugly*)

Here's a sign that should grab our attention:

BEWARE: RADIATION!

Maybe we should put it on the marketing department's door. When we're considering a prospect mailing for a store location, what will often be the first thing out of a marketer's mouth?

> *"Let's take the store's location and radiate out 3 or 5 or 10 miles. We'll find the people who look like our customers and we'll mail them an offer to visit the store."*

Hmm. Good luck with that.

Let's look at what might happen given a real case study. This location happens to be New York City, but the same principle applies in any area. We first defined the Trade Area for the store. Those zip codes, sales and customer count are represented in the leftmost columns below. The only difference between this and any other location in the US lies in the distances that one would need to radiate—it might be 3 miles in New York City, 5 to 10 miles in upstate New York, or 25 miles in Montana. Still, the principle remains the same.

Zips in the Store Trade Area

Rnk	Zip	Sales	Cust	Rad1	Rad2	Rad3	Rad4	Rad5
1	10012	$746,511	1,593	3,745	10,728	10,933	10,933	10,933
2	10003	$174,375	586		4,252	18,921	22,344	22,343
3	10011	$184,606	567		2	7,488	25,557	25,555
4	10013	$184,559	428		4,148	10,264	10,264	10,264
5	10014	$138,741	414		721	13,232	18,526	18,526
8	10016	$ 98,829	281				18,035	22,273
10	10010	$ 88,985	268				12,312	12,312
	Total	$2,136,854	5,967	3,745	23,558	99,740	210,433	358,560

In almost any location, it would be normal to expect that customers would travel as little as a couple of miles to patronize our store. Not so fast, my friends. Let the customers tell us how far they will travel and from where.

We'll start with the store location in zip code 10012 and radiate out some reasonable amount of distance from there, working with the population in each circle.

(Rad1) Radius #1: .25 miles around the store location

In a .25 mile circle around the store, there are about 3,745 mailable consumers. We should note that all of these people live inside zip code 10012. As we've already learned, inevitably the zip code where the store is constitutes the greatest concentration of our customers.

We could probably select all these records, send out a mail piece and count our money. Unfortunately, we need more than just 3,745 customers. 1,593 of these consumers are already our customer. The balance of this group is not inclined to visit our store—or they would have already been customers. They live within a quarter mile of the store. That's a driver and a nine iron.

(Rad2) Radius #2: .50 miles around the store location

Now, we're up to about 23,558 mailable consumers, and we're still on pretty safe ground. Notice that we picked up most of the balance of zip code 10012 and portions of other zip codes.

(Rad3) Radius #3: 1.00 miles around the store location

This is where the radiation method starts to fall apart.

The chart shows that for a 1 mile circle around the store, there are about 99,740 mailable consumers. However, in zip codes not shown on the chart above, we have consumers living within 1 mile of our store, who nevertheless are not in the Store Trade Area, defined by the zip code Concentration at the third column.

These folks may be our neighbors. But they're not our customers.

(Rad4) Radius #4: 2.00 miles around the store location

It's getting worse, not better. Here are 210,433 mailable consumers, but a large portion is in zip codes that never made it into the Store Trade Area.

(Rad5) Radius #5: 3.00 miles around the store location

> We might as well be in a foreign land. We have 358,560 mailable consumers, but an even larger portion is in zip codes outside the Store's Trade Area. In fact, 3 miles would take us over to Brooklyn and even into New Jersey.

So here we have the good, the bad and the ugly of the radiation method:

The Good—We did find our customers—or at least some of them. The top 5 zip codes, which make up about 47% of the store market area, are covered completely in the two or three mile radius.

The Bad—Many zip codes are covered that are not part of store trade area. It's not my job to determine why customers from these zip codes don't shop with us. It's my job to identify what's happening, and leverage that information in selecting the best prospects.

Like it or not, we're all creatures of convenience and habit. Most Brooklyn people don't want to come to Manhattan any more than Manhattan people want to go to Brooklyn to shop. Let's not even discuss people who live in New Jersey. I say this with impunity, as I lived there for 23 years, and still do part of the year.

The Ugly—Let's take one last look at the chart. Notice that from the list of top zip codes from the store trade area, Zip code ranking numbers 6, 7, 9, 11, and 12 (do not appear on the chart) are not included at all in the selection, even in the 2 or 3 mile circles. That's 22% of the store's trade area that is not represented in the radiation.

When it comes to finding our customers, the radiation method is a big net, pulling in some of what we want, plenty of what we don't want, and unfortunately, completely missing some of what we're after. As important as it is, we can't allow proximity (a radius) alone to define our customer base.

All month, we've been asking:

"Where Is Our Customer?"

We might think that we could safely include those who live within a couple miles of the store in our circle of customers. If we do, we're coming at the question from the wrong direction.

My Suggestion:

> **Allow your customer database to tell you where your customers come from.**

If we have our customers' addresses, we can construct Zip Code Concentration and Zip Code Penetration reports. We can narrow it down even further, to the exact Carrier Routes. Let's use this information to find our customers where they live, not where we choose to look for them.

Like a famous bank robber once said, "Go where the money is." In CRM, go where your current customers are and you're more likely to find new ones.

Chapter V

May—"Where, oh where has he gone?"

(Wk 1: Movers and shakers)

This month, we're still asking that same question: "**Where Are My Customers?**" But this time, we've got a different answer: **They're moving.**

Some customers are relocating a few blocks away. Some have switched states. Some have left the country completely. In their place, there are some new faces in town. Statistics tell us that 15–20 percent of the US population moves every year. If we're setting our sights on our customers, we'd better acknowledge that we're looking at a moving target.

Happily, tracking those wandering customers isn't as difficult as it might seem. Our friends at the post office have a method for telling us when our customers have moved, and where they went. **It's called the National Change of Address (NCOA).**

In the simplest of terms, NCOA is a big file of all the people who filled out those mover cards at the post office when they moved. Since about 40 million Americans change their address each year, and the post office has been doing this for several years, we can guess that the file is very large.

Not surprisingly, the post office has chosen not to perform the NCOA processing itself, but has instead licensed that function out to several different companies. All we need to do is to send our customer records to one of these organizations, and they will search to see if the customer has moved.

If they find that our customer has relocated, they will return the new address to us. Even better, unlike the person who keeps scribbling new phone numbers and addresses in the margins of my Filofax, these licensees use very exacting rules set up by the post office, to ensure they find the correct person. They don't want to tell us that someone moved if they did not.

Neat, huh? But what is all of this going to run us?

Answer: A lot less than mailing to the customer's old address. Think about it. Each time we lose track of our customer, we don't merely endure the cost of mailing to the incorrect address and having the piece trashed. We also suffer the expense of sales lost because our customer never received the mailing. This combination of costs easily justifies regularly sending our customer file out for NCOA processing.

I know too many retailers who stood idly by, watching the response to their direct mail events deteriorate significantly over time—simply because they wouldn't pay the relatively small price for NCOA. Once they understand the economics of the processing, and the damage done by not processing, most retailers become regular NCOA users.

One of my clients, who regularly sends their customer file out for NCOA processing, was able to identify, out of approximately 1 million customers, 38,874 customers who had moved. The chart below reflects the extent of the moves. What would we do if we knew who these customers were?

Cust Count	% of Total	Classification of Post-Move Status
17,153	44.1%	Same Store Trade Area
8,635	22.2%	One Store Trade Area to another
4,747	12.2%	Store Trade Area to Non-Trade Area
2,513	6.5%	Non-Trade Area to Store Trade Area
5,826	15.0%	Non-Trade Area to Non-Trade Area
38,874		**Total Number of NCOA Address Changes**

Once we get the NCOA file back, and our customer database is updated with new, corrected addresses, it's time to "mine the gold" that we find in them thar database "hills". Knowing our customer's post-move status gives us an opportunity to market to them before the competition in the new neighborhood does. However, we need to act quickly, wisely, and with as much information as we can muster.

My Suggestion:

If you're trying to hit a target that's always moving, you'd better keep moving as well.

Here's your first move: use the NCOA processing to keep your mailing records accurate and up to date. We can't afford to mail to customers at their old addresses. We really can't afford to lose customers every time they change their address. Unless we have a scheme to plant a homing device on our patrons, the NCOA statistics are the best method for keeping up with our "on the move" customers. Let's use it effectively, and frequently.

(Wk 2: Store trade area revisited)

Everyone has met a fisherman with a story of "the one that got away". But we retailers can go one better. Here's a story about the ones that got away.

Remember that snazzy illustration from last week's *Jem*, showing the breakdown of *classifications of Post-Move Status* for customers captured by the NCOA processing? Here it is again, for one more look:

Cust Count	% of Total	Classification of Post-Move Status
17,153	44.1%	Same Store Trade Area
8,635	22.2%	One Store Trade Area to another
4,747	12.2%	Store Trade Area to Non-Trade Area
2,513	6.5%	Non-Trade Area to Store Trade Area
5,826	15.0%	Non-Trade Area to Non-Trade Area
38,874		**Total Number of NCOA Address Changes**

Now how's this for a war story?

The retailer, whose data is represented on this chart, and in the following case study, has lost 11,000 customers who moved very quarter of the year. This makes a total loss for the year of 44,000 customers, averaging over 4 million dollars in annual sales.

Who can afford to lose over 44,000 customers per year?

This should get us thinking. Last week's *Jem* illustrated the importance of sending our database for NCOA processing on a regular basis. But after the housekeeping is complete, and we've made all the necessary address changes, what else should be done for our customers in each of the "Post-Move Status" categories?

First, we should understand how the lines are drawn between the categories. There's a phrase in those Classifications that should look familiar—it's "Store Trade Area". This is the area around a brick and mortar store, making up the largest portion of the customer base.

Store Trade Area: the geography around a store that includes approximately 80 percent of the customers who have purchased.

Not too surprisingly, this is the criterion we've used to breakdown our Post-Move statistics. Clearly, the Trade Area will never include every customer. Sometimes we get lucky, and a customer drops in while on vacation or a business trip. Accordingly, we wouldn't necessarily cut off all contact with a customer living outside the lines.

Generally speaking though, marketing to customers outside the Store Trade Area is not cost-effective. To justify marketing to a customer outside our choice geography, he or she would have to meet a more stringent criterion than a customer in our select zone; i.e., the customer may be required to have multiple transactions in order to be selected. Whoever said absence makes the heart grow fonder wasn't a retailer. For us, it's more like out of sight, out of mind.

Keep in mind that Post-Move statistics will look different for every retailer. However, every retailer will have all of the Post-Move Status categories represented. Obviously, the more stores a retailer has, the higher the probability that the customer's new address will be in a new store's Trade Area. As a result, the distribution of customers in each category will vary significantly from retailer to retailer, depending upon the number of locations, the size of the trade area, the product mix, the number of channels of distribution and a few other more minor factors.

Let's take a look at the case-study outlined in the graph above, and see if we can come up with a plan to reel in at least a few of those 44,000 customers about to slip away.

1. **17, 153 customers moved within the same store's trade area.** Many of these people may have moved across the street, to another part of town, or just changed apartments in the same complex. They've been patronizing one of our stores, and their move will probably not affect which store they patronize. Now that we have the new address information and can continue to be in contact, we can safely say: no harm done.

    In fact, depending on our store's product mix, there may be an opportunity waiting. As anyone who's ever gone through a move can attest, these customers have just had a temporary change in lifestyle. If we've got hardware, paint, wallpaper, furniture (or aspirin) in our product line, it's time for us to take quick action. Our communication should be planned in advance, so that as soon as an address change takes effect, a "trigger piece" will be in the mail. This chance won't last forever. Most of the expenditures in these merchandise categories peak during the first few months after the move. Let's move in, before the competition does.

2. **8,635 customers moved from Trade Area to Trade Area.** This is where most retailers miss the boat. Depending upon the size of our trade areas, this category represents customers who have moved from one zip code to another, from county to county, or state to state. Too often, these customers fall through the cracks and are left to fend for themselves.

I have seen retailers with Trade Areas containing hundreds of customers who, having recently moved into a new neighborhood, had no awareness of the store nearby. When accumulated across a chain of retail stores, these numbers can quickly turn into thousands of lost customers. If we don't make our presence known in the neighborhood, then only by accident will these people remain customers after moving. If we don't **communicate**, they won't come to the store.

This problem can be eliminated with relocation mailers. Again, we need some advance planning, so that the address change immediately triggers a mail piece that will:

- Acknowledge the customer's move
- Invite the customer into the new store
- Let the customer know where the store is
- Give them an incentive to visit.

Like the little old lady next door, who shows up at the door with a basket of cookies, our message is: "welcome to the neighborhood."

3. **4,747 customers moved from Trade Area to Non-Trade Area.** These are customers who simply moved to a location that is not in any of our stores' Trade Areas. This does not make them bad people. It doesn't mean that we will never talk to them again. But it does mean that they will have to pass some tests in order to justify our marketing efforts to them.

If our only channel of distribution is retail, we'll need to see if they continue to purchase, despite living outside the store's trade area. Then, we can respond accordingly. If we also have catalog and/or web sales as a channel, we can always remind the customer that the same great products/services are available in the catalog or on our website.

4. **2,513 customers moved from Non-Trade Area to Trade Area.** Well, look who just stepped off the bus ... These are customers who used to live in the hinterlands, or at least outside our trade area, but have now moved into our neck of the woods. Most of the time, this group is not large in number. Still, they should receive the same warm welcome as any customer moving into a new trade area.

5. **5,826 customers moved from Non-Trade Area to Non-Trade Area.** There's not too much for us to do with these. Again, for the relocation marketing efforts to be cost effective, these customers will have to meet more stringent selection criteria. Depending on our channels of distribution, product line, and what we learn by tracking sales, we'll see whether this customer should stay on our marketing list.

NCOA statistics are one of the most misunderstood and most underutilized resources in the marketing industry. They can tell us which of our customers have recently moved—and even better; they can tell us where they've gone. Once we know that, we can use our knowledge of our stores' trade areas to find the best course of action for retaining each category of customer.

My Suggestion:

> **If your customers are moving (and they are), then don't just stand there. Do something!**

Create a communication strategy in advance, for those moving within your trade area or to a new trade area. Don't let your customers get away!

(Wk 3: Truth, justice and the NCOA way)

As the Seeker of Truth and Wisdom ascended the mountain, he saw the old wise man sitting cross-legged, in front of a cave. "You have come a great distance, my son," said the old man. "You may ask me your questions, and I shall answer you."

The Seeker quickly caught his breath, and approached the old man. "I ... I have only one question", he stammered. "If 15–20 percent of the US population moves every year, and the post office has a method of finding those people, why are companies so averse to sending out their files for National Change of Address processing?"

The old man fell silent, lost in thought. Without a word, he rose, and disappeared into his cave. Seconds later, he returned carrying a worn, tattered book. On the front, it said: *Jems from Johnson*. He dusted it off and read for a few minutes. Then he closed the book. He looked up at the young man.

> "I don't know," said the wise man, shaking his head. "No one knows. NCOA processing is simple and very inexpensive compared to the benefits derived." He shrugged his shoulders. "Go figure".

More than 50% of data warehouse projects have limited success due to their lack of addressing data quality issues.

Customer Relationship Management is definitely a data warehouse project. An address to which a mail piece cannot be delivered would definitely be a data quality issue. If we can improve our data quality by simply sending the file out for NCOA, why not do it and do it often?

The post office requires semi-annual processing of NCOA in order for a sender to take advantage of the postal discounts. Many retailers use that post office requirement as an excuse to only process NCOA every 6 months. But if 15–20 percent of the population moves every year, then about 7 to 10 percent move every 6 months.

Do we really think all those people waited to move until the day before we sent our file out for NCOA? Many of them moved the day after we last sent our file. We've been mailing to them with no result for the past 6 months.

In addition to returning address changes, the NCOA processors return error codes for records that should be flagged for "no future mailings". These codes include:

1. **Moved. No Forwarding Address.** The addressee has changed residences, but has not filled out that little change of address form at the Post Office.

2. **Box Closed.** Not necessarily an indication that the addressee has moved, but simply an announcement that the person is no longer receiving mail at this PO Box.

3. **Foreign Move.** There's not much point in mailing customers who have moved to foreign countries. Do we really think a customer now living in Portugal will fly over for the biggest Mother's Day Sale on Earth?

4. **Address Could Not Be Confirmed.** The address on the change of address form could not be confirmed. If the address isn't accurate, we don't want it. This exercise is all about data quality.

I encourage my clients to process AT LEAST every 3 months, but sometimes to no avail. Many larger clients have been persuaded to process every month due to the volume of address changes they are finding. If the post office required processing every 3 months, it would make all retailers improve their data quality, while also making the post office more efficient. Still, so many retailers, citing the costs of NCOA processing, stick with the bare minimum 6 month regimen.

Ever hear of the saying "penny wise and pound foolish"? Take a look at this case study: Having tracked NCOA results for many retailers over a long period of time, I can tell you that the percentage of records indicating a recent move, or one of the other error code conditions, hovers around 1.5 percent per month. So:

> If processed every 6 months, it is around 9–10 percent.
> If processed every 3 months, it is around 4.5–5 percent.
> If processed every month, it is around 1.5–2 percent.

Okay, okay. I realize that it costs 6 times as much to process every month as it does to process every 6 months. Here's the question:

> What does it cost us to wait 6 months, while a portion of our mail pieces are, literally and figuratively, lost in space?

If we have a file of 200,000 customer records, which we can process for a minimum of $500 each time (larger volumes will derive volume discounts), then our NCOA cost is $500 every six months.

Consider the hidden costs of not processing:

Let's start by noting that the number of customers who have moved during those 6 months will grow, right along with the cost of having mailed to them. Assuming a $.40 per piece cost for creative, printing, and mailing, the total cost of mailing to these bad addresses is over $25,000 during the 6 months. That's the sum of mailing costs, and the cost of finding out which addresses are wrong.

> "Yes, yes. Of course. But I wouldn't mail to people who have moved. What a waste of money...."

Mmm. Exactly. Except that we don't know who moved until we process the NCOA. In fact, for six months, we've been doing exactly that—sending to people who are no longer there.

On the other hand, what would it cost to process NCOA every month?

We'd be looking at $3,000 for the 6 NCOA processes. On the other hand, we would know which of our customers had relocated after just 1 month. Subsequently, our cost of mailing bad addresses would drop to $7,200. This makes our total cost $10,200.

There we have it: a savings of about $15,000 or $30,000 annually.

Why am I beating my head against the wall here? It makes so much economic sense!!

My Suggestion:

> **You can't afford to wait for a half a year to find out where your customers have gone.**

NCOA processing will always be less expensive than mailing to the wrong address. Send your files out for processing every 1–3 months.

(Wk 4: Movers ARE shakers—new customers)

So when was the last time you moved? No—not from the couch and the remote control. When was the last time you *changed locations*?

If you are like the rest of America, you relocate an average of once every five years. In fact, about 15 to 20 percent of the US population moves every year. Maybe that's why we've spent this month discussing the challenges of keeping up with our constantly moving customer. Maybe that's why we should end the month thinking about the opportunities these movers and shakers represent.

If no one ever moved, we would not have a group of fresh prospects from which to glean new customers. If no one ever moved, all those people living in our store's trade area who haven't stepped into the store would continue not stepping in. At least when these non-customers finally move out of the neighborhood, someone new will take their place. Perhaps that someone will become our customer.

As the shark said to the stranger who swam by: "We could use some new blood around here".

In the CRM industry, these new arrivals in the neighborhood are known as **New Movers**—and they are terrific candidates for becoming our future loyal customers. How terrific? Let's take a look:

Approximately 1.3 million households move each year. Granted, only a small portion will actually move into our store market area, unless we are Starbucks and have a coffee shop on every corner. Most retailers' store trade areas, when taken in total, make up a very small portion of the US geography.

Admittedly, we are talking about small numbers on a monthly basis. Don't let that deter you in marketing to New Movers. The value isn't in how many. It's in how much.

> **Each of these New Mover households spends on average $10–12,000 more than their neighbors during the first year after relocating.**

It sounds like a lot of money. But have you moved recently? My wife and I recently rented an apartment in the New York area. For weeks, every time Tina left the apartment, she returned with a carload of stuff. These were not welcome gifts from friendly neighbors. This was hundreds of dollars worth of merchandise, purchased from stores in the immediate area.

Now we happen to be familiar with the area, so we pre-selected some of the stores that Tina patronized. But what if we had not known the area? Tina is a world-class shopper—she would certainly have found somewhere to spend all that money.

A Quote from my wife Tina: "EXCUSE ME.... I GUESS WE DIDN'T NEED THOSE FRIVOLOUS THINGS LIKE SHEETS, TOWELS, FOOD, DISHES, AND SWEATERS FOR COLD WEATHER!"

When new customers show up on our doorstep, as retailers, it's our job to **communicate** and make our presence known. Don't think that New Movers will take the time to seek us out. They have better things to do.

Likewise, don't assume that they will take the time to comparative shop our store and our biggest competitor in the area. These people are living in a house filled with boxes; Great Grandma Edna's heirloom porcelain piece is broken into twenty pieces; Dad can't remember where he packed his passport. Moving is not easy. There's a lot on their minds.

Consequently, we can provide a service by communicating to these New Movers immediately after they arrive in the neighborhood. We can't wait for them to find us. They need us to find them.

Where do we get the names and addresses of these new movers?

Well, we could chase after every moving van passing through the neighborhood. Or instead, we could work with some companies that acquire this information for us. They do it all day long. They are very good at it. They acquire it from a variety of sources, including listings of new telephone connections, then they sell the names and addresses of these New Movers at anywhere from $100–$200 per 1,000 names.

Why such a great variance in cost?

It's all in the timing. The fresher the name, the more expensive the list will be. These companies provide a weekly hotline (just arrived in the neighborhood) at a better than 50 percent premium over the 30-day hotline. The 30-day hotline versus the 60-day (not so hotline) is a 15 percent premium.

They know something that we should know. There is a sizeable benefit to contacting the New Mover as quickly as possible. In this case, the early bird really does get the worm. We want to be the first in the mailbox for a New Mover, even if we must pay more for that opportunity.

Should we go out and buy all the New Movers in a 10 mile radius of our store?

Of course not. Let's use our database. First, we can see which zip codes have the highest concentration of current customers (that old Trade Area thing again). Then we can pick the top 10 zip codes and find the New Movers in those selected areas. It will cost another $5–10 premium per 1,000 consumers for the zip code selection, but our response and ROI will increase accordingly.

Likewise, if the third party data provider allows for demographic selects, we can also use that criterion. Let's identify the demographics of our best customers, and target those New Movers who match up. For example, if our best customers are females aged 20–30, we would not want to target middle-aged couples moving into the neighborhood.

Why **Movers and Shakers** this month? Maybe it's because Tina and I had just rented that apartment in New York. Perhaps it's because spring and summer are the most active moving months. If we don't jump on the bandwagon now to **communicate** with New Movers in our store trade area, we will have an even smaller group of New Movers in the fall.

Customers are not the only things always moving. So is time. If we don't act immediately, we'll lose both of them.

My Suggestion:

Don't miss a chance to capture the new kids on the block.

Using a third party service provider, and your own database information, you can find the names and addresses of New Movers who look like your customers. Then, get a *Welcome to the Neighborhood* event mailer into their hands—and do it fast. One good move deserves another.

Chapter VI

June—Follow the bouncing customer

(Wk 1: FIRST (not the third) time's the charm)

And so the summer begins. No Monday morning meeting this week, I suppose. I hope everyone enjoyed their Memorial Day holiday.

Although I did end my formal schooling more than a few years ago, I still recall the feeling of the first day of summer vacation—that heady anticipation of a whole season of freedom lying ahead. That's the feeling I had when I was nine years old, on a June morning just like this—the first official day of summer break. I ran downstairs and sat down at the breakfast table to plan the day's activities. My mother looked over at me …

"What are those red dots on your skin?" she asked.

Chickenpox—on the first day of summer: it's always important to get off to a good start.

On that note, let's start this month by asking ourselves a question:

What is the most important transaction in the lifecycle of our customer?

- A sales person might decide that it's the transaction where the customer spent the most money. That lucky salesperson scored a big SPIFF on that visit.

- A store buyer might choose the transaction where the customer bought those slow-moving shoes that no one else would buy. Those shoes deserved a "Longevity" award. They'd been around longer than most of the staff.

- A marketer has to like that clearance sale transaction—the one when the customer responded to the mail piece, and took advantage of the special season-end incentive.

Those are all *memorable* transactions. But we'll never have those memories if we don't properly handle **the first transaction**. That's the most important transaction in the customer's lifecycle.

The Direct Marketing Association says that more than 50 percent of first-time customers never return to purchase the second time. This statistic proves true across all types of retailers. In fact, I have found the statistic to be even higher than 50 percent for specialty store retailers.

Talk about getting off to a poor start:

- Across the industry, more than half of first-time shoppers who purchase … **never returned for a second transaction.**

- Think of all the expenditures for advertising and marketing. More than half the first-time shoppers … **never returned for a second transaction.**

- Think of the expense of researching and finding the right store location. More than half of the first-time shoppers … **never returned for a second transaction.**

- Think of all the cost for hiring, staff training, product design, and inventory. More than half of the first-time shoppers … **never returned for a second transaction.**

Just so you know that I'm not blowing smoke, let me tell you: I've had clients where the repurchase rate for first-time purchasers, before Claude Johnson Associates worked it's magic, ranged from 18 percent to about 38 percent. There was lots of room for improvement.

If you prefer to see the glass as half empty—well, it's actually more than half empty. The percentage of new customers who never return for a second transaction ranges from 50–82. Welcome to the land of lost profits!!!

Is the First Transaction a problem or an opportunity? It all depends on what we do with it. If we persist in believing that every first-time customer loves us (who wouldn't?), and is naturally devoted to us for life, we definitely have a problem.

On the other hand, if we're willing to acknowledge the challenge, and take steps to address it, we might have just found ourselves a goldmine. If we approach the First-Time Shopper strategically, he or she represents a prime opportunity to increase sales.

Historically, retailers have used 4 money-eating tactics in their endless attempts to increase sales:

1. **Opening more stores.** It's costly, time consuming and doesn't address customer retention.

2. **Increasing demand.** Advertising, price promotion, and marketing efforts are expensive and difficult to measure.

3. **Hiring more sales people.** This isn't cheap either. Then we have to train the new employees to deliver a shopping experience that will compel customers to come back.

4. **Investing in inventory, supply chain.** This means hiring more buyers, and training everyone in the company to meet the challenge of the core customer.

What if instead we put our efforts into developing programs to better service the customers who've already visited our store? More specifically, what if we could move the needle in persuading our newest customers, those First-Time Shoppers, to return for another visit? For most retailers, more than 50 percent of transactions are with new customers. If we can win over our First-Time Shoppers, we could transform our sales results.

What is the financial impact on getting the first transaction right? Here is an actual case study from a small retail client of mine.

160,000	Annual New Customer Count
$ 50.00	Average First Transaction Amount (Sales)
$ 71.50	Average Second Transaction Amount (Sales)
$156.00	Average Spend over the next 12 months (Net Sales)

The client, a specialty retailer, acquires 160,000 new customers per year. The average spend for the first transaction is $50. For those who return to buy a second time, the second transaction averages $71.50. On average, those return customers spend $156 over the next twelve months. The moral of the story:

Customers who know you, and like you, will return to spend more.

Out of the 160,000 annual new customers, this retailer recorded a 38 percent repurchase rate over the 12 months following the first transaction. The total New

Customer sales for the 12 months following the first transaction were about $9.5 million (this includes the second and subsequent transactions).

38% of First Time Buyers Return in 12 Months

$3,040,000	Second Transaction Sales
$4,347,200	All Additional Transaction Sales
$9,484,800	Annual Sales for Returning First Time Buyers

If we could get one additional First-Time Shopper to come back for a second transaction, we would increase annual sales by $156. If we could develop a program to increase the number of First-Time Shoppers returning for an additional visit by just one percent, it would generate $249,000 in incremental sales. Imagine if we could increase the return rate by 5 percent. We would create $1.2 million in incremental sales.

Increase 1%

1,600	Incremental—New Customers Returning
$ 114,400	Incremental—New Customers Return Sales
$ 249,600	Incremental—Annual sales for new customers
	Who return for a second transaction

Increase 5%

8,000	Incremental—New Customers Returning
$ 572,000	Incremental—New Customers Return Sales
$ 1,248,000	Incremental—Annual sales for new customers
	Who return for a second transaction

Increase 10%

16,000	Incremental—New Customers Returning
$ 572,000	Incremental—New Customers Return Sales
$ 2,496,000	Incremental—Annual sales for new customers
	Who return for a second transaction

Does it sound farfetched? How would we like an increase of 10 percent, or $2.5 million in incremental sales? That is exactly what we did working with one of our clients. They increased their first transaction customer return rate by 10 percentage points. I love this job.

What did we do to get more customers to return after their first transaction?

We didn't run more full-page ads in the newspapers.
We didn't hire new salespeople.
We didn't build more stores.
We didn't invest in more inventory for the stores.

We developed a program to address the customer after he or she left the store. We've already discussed the importance of capturing customer data correctly on the first visit. Our post transaction effort is just as important. So let's spend June looking at how to get off on the right foot—what to do after the first transaction, to get that First-Time Shopper back for a repeat performance.

My Suggestion:

> **Don't limit your attention to large, memorable transactions, no matter how big or well-timed they may be.**

The most important transaction is the first one, and the most efficient way to improve sales is to raise the percentage of repurchases from your new customers.

My daddy, who did not raise any dummies (except maybe a few of my siblings), said:

"You can't get a third transaction without the second one". Loyalty is built one step at a time, and it starts right after that first transaction.

(Wk 2: Repurchase facts)

Still thinking about that 10 percent increase in the repurchase rate of New Customers that I cited last week? Did you do the calculations, to know what even a minimal increase in New Customer repurchases could mean to your sales?

If your first customer transaction averages $100 and all other metrics applied, the following incremental sales would be generated for:

> 1 percent increase = $.5 million incremental sales
>
> 5 percent increase = $2.5 million incremental sales
>
> 10 percent increase = $5.0 million incremental sales

Anyone not interested in picking up an extra 5 million dollars in sales can take the week off. The rest of us are going to take a look at a case study to see what a real, living, breathing client did when they recognized the importance of that First Transaction. Let's go to Glik's ...

Glik Stores is a 109 years old, family-managed company in the Midwest with 55 family apparel stores. Prior to getting CRM religion, Glik's spent a very large portion of their marketing budget on newspaper and radio advertising.

When I analyzed their customer database, I discovered that only 39 percent of more than 100,000 annual New Customers returned to purchase again, in the 24 months after their first purchase. That 24 month period is a pretty wide window. If the customer hasn't returned in two years, they aren't coming back without being hog-tied and dragged to the store (which is one of the few CRM strategies that Claude Johnson Associates does not embrace).

This repurchase rate came as something of a surprise to Glik's management. After all, this is a "customer-first" retailer, located in small, rural towns in the Midwest, where "we know everyone, and they know us." In fact, our tests showed that the store managers at Glik's know their best customers between 90–100 percent of the time.

Yet despite all that personalized customer service, the stores had never formalized a program for their new customers. The challenge was to translate the customer's first store experience into a continuing relationship.

We discovered the following metrics for Glik's New Customers:

First-Time Shoppers (annualized)	100,000
First transaction sales (annualized)	$4,649,631
Average First Transaction value	$46.50
Repurchase Rate (24 months)	39.0%
Lifetime value of those	
Who did repurchase in 24 months	$9,121,215
Average Lifetime Value	$233.88

Once again, we could look at these numbers and see a problem, or an opportunity. Happily, Glik's management group saw the potential. If we could increase the repurchase rate even a little, it would generate big gains in lifetime sales (which we have defined here as the next 24 months for First-Time Shoppers). A repurchase rate increase of 1 percent would result in an increase of over $90,000 in sales. A more respectable 10 percent increase would create an additional $900,000 in 24 months sales from First-Time Shoppers.

The smart quarterback of the Glik's team, Jeff Glik himself, didn't expect to win the Super Bowl with the first play of the season. He asked us to design a new customer program, use it as a learning vehicle for his company, and to refine it after we monitored the results. No one finds a perfect solution, instantly. Ideas are refined into solutions. Smart retailers allow for a learning curve.

The first step in the process was to name this program. Glik's called it: **Newly Created Customers**. There's a message in that name. If we have a First-Time Shopper whose name and address record does not make it into our database, we don't have a new customer.

Like the proverbial tree in the forest that no one can hear, a new customer for whom we fail to obtain a name and address falls outside of our program. Glik's understood that we must *create a customer* from a First-Time Shopper, and we begin that process by obtaining the all-important information for the database.

The second step in the program was to distinguish First-Time Shoppers from other customers. We wanted to send a targeted message only to this segment of customers. Our strategy required a monthly review of New Customer transactions. Each of these names would then receive a very simple postcard in the mail.

As these postcards were Glik's first venture into CRM, the early versions didn't do much more than **communicate** an offer to the customer in a timely manner. Later, the postcards became increasingly lively and creative. According to our friends at the Direct Marketing Association, three primary factors impact response to direct mail, in varying degrees:

> 50 percent of the response rate depends on the list.
> 40 percent of the response rate depends on the offer.
> 10 percent of the response rate depends on the creative.

So how did we do at Glik's?

Initially, we worked on selecting the list of new customers. As per the data above, this is where most of the impact would come from in a direct mail campaign.

The response rates ranged from 8–15 percent in the first 6–9 months, tracking higher during the seasonal shopping spikes. These were pretty impressive returns, and the success was shared throughout the company. Even more importantly, the promotions lifted the percentage of the First-Time Shoppers who become regular customers.

With all of that accomplished, the final challenge was to refine our approach. Glik's CFO wanted to "best utilize the expenditure" of this program. Does your CFO talk like that? This meant breaking down the Newly Created Customer population into smaller, measurable categories, to discover which segments out-performed the others.

We immediately recognized that the dollar value of the first transaction was an indicator of return rate, as well as a gauge of the lifetime value of the customer. The chart below reflects Newly Created Customers for the month of March, tracked for the next 24 months.

First Transaction Dollar Value

Monetary Distribution	# of Cust	Trans Dollars	Next 24 Months Cust	Rate
$$0	167	$ -	46	27.2%
$1–25	3,887	$ 60,003	1,869	48.1%
$26–50	3,428	$124,295	1,851	54.0%
$51–100	2,539	$168,245	1,446	56.9%
$101–150	704	$ 83,075	436	61.9%
$151–200	238	$ 40,002	147	61.8%
$201+	165	$ 41,722	106	64.4%
Total	11,127	$517,341	5,899	53.0%

It's interesting to notice in the first row that 46 of the 167 customers who had an even exchange ($0) on their initial transaction, ultimately returned to buy more (27.2%). This shows that even those who initially bought nothing (that is purchased and returned) will come back, but at a relatively low rate. Not too surprisingly, the larger the initial transaction, the higher the probability is of a return purchase.

By setting a minimum threshold on the first transaction value, we were able to increase the return on investment and reduce the total cost of the program, while optimizing results.

First Transaction Dollar Value

Monetary Distribution	# of Cust	Trans Dollars	Lifetime Sales	Avg	Trans
$$0	167	$ -	$ 4,907	$107.84	4.67
$1–25	3,887	$ 60,003	$ 297,351	$159.10	5.23
$26–50	3,428	$124,295	$ 380,932	$205.86	5.52
$51–100	2,539	$168,245	$ 395,390	$273.53	5.90
$101–150	704	$ 83,075	$ 156,292	$358.88	6.30
$151200	238	$ 40,002	$ 75,707	$515.01	7.57
$201+	165	$ 41,722	$ 69,064	$651.55	7.94
Total	11,127	$517,341	$1,379,642	$233.88	5.67

From the chart, you can see that any customer who spent over $200 in the first purchase is four times as valuable as a customer who spent $25 in the first purchase. By targeting the most responsive customers, and the most valuable ones, we were able to significantly increase our ROI.

My Suggestion:

> Put a program in place to target First Time Shoppers with a simple mail piece.

That will reinforce their shopping experience with us, and encourage them to visit again soon. Then, go one step further to maximize your results, by directing your efforts to the customers most likely to respond with a significant purchase.

The Bard tells us that "All's well that ends well." Maybe. But Johnson (and I don't mean Samuel) tells us that "All's well that begins well." Customers are like hot dogs. We 'gotta get 'em while they're hot.'

(Wk 3: First impressions)

Anyone who's ever interviewed for a job or gone on a blind date has learned the lesson:

First impressions matter—because you only get one chance to make them.

Since we're spending the month of June thinking about opportunities to maximize the value of First Transactions, we should be sure that our approach to First-Time Shoppers is not only about selling. It should also be about telling—conveying our brand's image and message to our new customer, as quickly and clearly as possible.

Let's remember that over half of our new purchasers never return to the store. If we're going to send a message, we'd better do it as soon as possible after that first transaction. For at least some segment of our First-Time Shoppers, there will not be a second or third opportunity to do it. Speak now, or forever hold your mail piece.

Last week, we looked at how Glik Stores went about targeting their **Newly Created Customers** with an incentive to return to the store. This week, let's examine how they embraced the other challenge—sending that customer not just an invitation to return, but an explanation of what Glik's is all about. It's not just a matter of what we say. It's also a matter of who we are, and how we introduce ourselves.

When Mr. Glik opened his first store 109 years ago, he sold apparel to the families in town. Every new transaction with a customer provided Mr. Glik an opportunity to "tell his retail story." He could do it face to face with the shoppers. From that single store, this man and his heirs expanded to 55 stores, selling apparel to families in 54 other towns.

How can Glik's tell that same story to customers in 55 stores across five states? How do they explain what sets Glik's apart from all of the competition? This is a tough challenge for most retailers. In a competitive, information-saturated environment, how do we **communicate** our identity? What's our story, and how and when should we tell it?

Remember our "unique selling proposition"? Those words were pounded into all of us during the 1980's. Our unique proposition is simply whatever it is that makes us special to our customers. While we may know it, and our loyal customers may know it, our First-Time Shoppers do not.

Before they bought something from us, these first-timers were someone else's "best customer". Now that they've happened to find us, will they shop our entire store, investigate our history, learn our pricing strategy, examine our merchandise presentation and in general, discover what sets us apart from the competition? It's not very likely. It's probably better that we tell them.

Actually, let's start by showing them. After all, actions speak louder, and don't require mailing. We'll hope that the customer's initial shopping experience in our store demonstrated the story we'd like to tell.

With that accomplished, we should immediately reinforce that experience with a welcoming mail or email promotion. We have a very narrow window of opportunity, and this is it. If we don't do it after that first transaction, we probably won't get another chance. The sooner we do it, the better.

That's what Jeff Glik, president of Glik's, and I discovered through trial and error. Looking back, I probably should have known that immediate response to the customer would be much more effective than a delayed one. Unfortunately, CRM knowledge is rarely endowed at birth. Most of us mortals have to live and learn.

We also have to learn, over time, how to best tell our story in that all-important first approach. It must be done subtly, largely through images, with only a few choice words that convey what our company is all about. We shouldn't be surprised if it takes some refining. Someone asked a famous author what a good writer does that a novice does not do. The well-known writer answered: "Rewrite".

Jeff has been gracious enough to share some of his various efforts at telling the Glik's story to their new customers. Here briefly is Glik's evolution, beginning with their first Newly Created Customer postcard.

Overall, it's not a bad first effort. It's certainly better than no effort at all. But it doesn't fully succeed at conveying the identity of Glik's. The creative approach is generic, with no targeted message, and no real story being told.

With a little experience under their belt, Glik's eventually realized that the postcard was their chance to reinforce the family shopping experience for their Newly Created Customers. So they changed their postcard to deliver this message: *"Glik's is a family owned retailer, managed by the original family ..., selling to families in the Midwest."*

It's the same offer, but now every detail of the card reinforces Glik's unique selling proposition. All of the people on the postcard are Glik's family members, wearing products sold in the stores. In fact, for their own family holiday cards, the Glik's just enclose one of these postcards, so grandpa can see the latest picture of his grandchildren. If they need more models, they bring in family friends.

There are seasonal versions of the postcards with different products. For Mother's Day, the Glik's mothers and their children are presented. For Father's Day, the Glik's fathers and their children take a turn in the spotlight.

These pictures are indeed worth a thousand words. They convey that Glik's customers are men, women and children. The whole approach sends a very subtle, but powerful message: the Glik family provides your family all the apparel you want.

My Suggestion:

Make that opening line count.

Don't contact your First-Time Shoppers only to offer an incentive. Offer an identity. You need to act fast, and tell your new customers who you are, and what makes your store special.

(Wk 4: Catch (capture) that bouncing ball)

1. When do we make our first contact with a new customer? Naturally, it's during the first sales transaction.

2. When is our first opportunity to capture the customer's name and address? Again, it's during that first sales transaction.

3. When do we want to capture the customer data correctly: At the FIRST sales transaction! In the words of Homer Simpson: "Duh".

4. Sometimes it's not just what we do. It's how we do it. Let's do it right the first time.

If we can capture the customer data correctly at the first transaction, our chances are very good that the data will remain correct for the entire lifecycle of the customer. We might spend a little more time and money getting things right on that first encounter. But the payoff will come during all the subsequent transactions.

We can't market to our customers if we don't know where and how to contact them. If only half of our First Time Shoppers will ever come back for another visit, then at least half of the time, that First Transaction is our only chance to get the information right. There's not much margin for error.

Ever heard of GIGO? It means: "Garbage In … Garbage Out". It is pretty expensive garbage when the information captured at POS is invalid and the customer cannot be contacted. I work with my clients in a never-ending battle to analyze, identify, and correct customer database errors. Frankly, most of the time, it's a losing war. It's often impossible to correct the errors, even if they could all be detected.

Wouldn't it be better to correct the errors before they get into the system?

When we get the customer data right, we don't just save the expense of bad mailing and lost business. Consider the hidden benefits:

• Increased confidence across the organization that the database is correct and ready for use.

• Increased probability that duplicate customer records will be properly identified and the transactions merged. This is how to make good customers into better customers.

- If the license cost of the database software is governed by the number of customer records, we can increase our yield for that software asset and delay the capital cost to upgrade our license to the next level.

- When appending additional information to the customer records, the accuracy of the effort is increased, thereby increasing the yield on customer appending expenses.

Needless to say, there's not much argument here. It pays to get things right the first time. Nevertheless, that 5 percent error rate can be a stubborn barrier to break. There's always that little nuisance known as human fallibility.

No one means to get customer data wrong. What we need is a helping hand—a software that can help us correctly enter the mailing address, phone number, and email address at the point of sale register, on the web, or at the catalog order desk.

After much searching, Claude Johnson Associates finally found that software provider a couple of months ago. **QAS POS software does only one thing: the entry of correct mailing addresses.** But it's done well, and that's enough.

QAS turned our heads with these features:

- It's very user friendly and easy to install.
- When the address is entered, it is valid.
- It reduces key strokes by as much as two-thirds.
- It has the same features for Web, Catalog and POS Registers

What common mistakes can be caught by this software?

Point of Sale

- Bad zip code/city/state combination
- Incorrect or missing directional like N or S
- Misspelling of the address
- Missing or invalid apartment numbers

Web

It is normally expected that customer-entered data is correct. WRONG. Not all web-shoppers are great data entry clerks. Some are still thrown by the slightest computer hiccup. All of the problems found at point of sale are often more prevalent on the web.

Catalog Order Center

Add a new problem to our list: Misunderstood voice communication. What was that? Some folks can't understand Claude Johnson's Southern accent, even though he's lived north of the Mason-Dixon Line for five decades now.

Off-site Data Entry Facility

(usually for loyalty card or private credit applications).
You thought Claude's speech was hard to understand. You should see his handwriting. Here's another hurdle to get over.

My Suggestion:

If you're going to target First-Time Shoppers, start by getting the name and address right.

Think about using the QAS software, to improve your best efforts at accuracy. Let's use any means necessary to increase our chances of capturing our new customer's data correctly once and for all time. We don't always get a second chance.

(Wk 5: Three "R's" of retail)

Back in the 70's and 80's, those good old days of retailing, success was all a matter of the "3 Rights". No—not Life, Liberty, and Happiness. Our merchant forefathers bequeathed to us a different set of rights:

The *right merchandise* in the *right place* at the *right price*.

Those were the days. Retailers were dominated by product-oriented thinking. However, as my kids occasionally point out to me, times do change. Now, inventory management is a given. Today, in order to be successful, we must send:

The **right message** to the **right customer** at the **right time**.

This doesn't eliminate the need for the right merchandise, in the right place, at the right price. Those are unalienable, as they say. But product alone will no longer do the job. Now it matters what we say, to whom we say it, and as we've been discussing all this month, *when we say it …*

From the modern political campaign, we've all learned the importance of staying "on message", which usually translates to hammering home the same point with unwavering consistency. If only our politicians were as dedicated to figuring out *what* to say, before they said it over and over again.

For the retailer, our message to the First-Time Shopper is pretty clear. "Thanks for your recent purchase" should work just fine. If we're positive that it is indeed the customer's first purchase, then we can even venture so far as "Thanks for your first purchase". This works especially well for web/catalog sales, where all transactions are tracked to the customer. Those of us surrounded by brick and mortar might not be confident enough to send so precise a message.

It's also not too tough to know who we should say this to. Clearly, the "right customer" is the one who has just shopped with us for the first time.

But when is the *right time* for our communication to the new customers? If we've been paying attention to the *Jems* of June, this shouldn't stump anyone, either. As Paul Revere warned that the British were coming, we should be sending this message ASAP. Our communication needs to happen as soon as possible after the first transaction.

If we've acquired the customer's email address during his or her first transaction, our new customer message can literally be immediate. Isn't it impressive when you receive automatic email acknowledgement messages from web sites, filtered by your stated interests or triggered by web purchases? It warms a CRM man's heart.

If we've acquired the customer's telephone number, but not the email address, the new customer message can be transmitted in a matter of minutes via voice messaging, again filtered by the customer's stated interests.

The dilemma is: not many shoppers will voluntarily give their name, address, email address, and telephone number on their first visit to a store.

Luckily, we don't need everything at once. This is the start of a relationship. Some of my clients capture customer information on 85–90 percent of all transactions, including new, First-Time Shoppers. They do it by starting with the name and address during the first transaction, then filling in the phone and email as things develop over the next few months. Don't be a hog on the first transaction. We just need some way to be in touch.

Once we have name and addresses, we have three effective techniques available to acknowledge our new customers:

1. A thank you note from the sales person
2. A thank you postcard from the home office
3. A Welcome Package for a store Loyalty Program

The first two hardly require explanation. While gratitude may be an endangered species, it's not yet extinct. We know how to say thanks. The Loyalty Program Welcome Package explains the rules of the program, customer rights and privileges, and typically extends an offer to shop again soon. This is simple stuff. Like I said, our challenge is not what to say. It's **WHEN** to say it.

Too often, the timing of these communications is dictated by the economies of monthly production cycles for selecting, printing and mailing the piece. Of course, the cost of a monthly production cycle is less than the cost for a bi-weekly or weekly schedule.

But it's not all a matter of costs. We can't know which schedule is more cost-effective until we see the response rate for a one-week turnaround, compared to that of a monthly cycle. After all, if our only consideration was to reduce the costs for creative and mailing, we could send our communications quarterly, or maybe just skip them all together. Don't let the CFO see that suggestion.

The chart below shows the actual results for one of my clients monthly mailings to new customers. Using the "lowest cost method wins" approach to marketing, monthly was the best frequency that could be negotiated with the finance department.

This client has a very structured new customer program: In the first week of the month, they select the list of new customers from the previous month. Then, this data is sent over to the mail house and mailed third class. Keep in mind that if we send a postcard immediately after the transaction via third class mail, our customer receives it nine days later. That doesn't exactly convey a sense of urgency to get the mailer in the hands of the customer, does it?

Elapsed time for the entire process: 5–7 weeks, from the customer's first transaction to the receipt of the communication, depending upon the purchase date during the previous month. By that time, many busy customers will have forgotten who the retailer is.

I've titled this 5–7 week time span, **TLTTD (Total Length of Time from Transaction to Delivery.)** Catchy isn't it? Sounds like a florist commercial.

This **TLTTD** *is not our friend.* If the right time to trigger a customer communication is immediately after the transaction, then certainly the optimal time for the customer to receive the communication would not be seven weeks later. The biggest factor in determining the response rate for a mail piece is the length of the **TLTTD**, the total length of time between the transaction and the delivery of the message to the customer.

What if, instead of monthly mailings, we decided to pull the list every two weeks, print, and mail first class. This would reduce the **TLTTD** from 5–7 weeks to 3–3.5 weeks. The mailing has the same message, same offer, same creative, same selection criteria, except it's done every 2 weeks rather than monthly. Will it cost more? Of course, it will. Is the investment worth it? You betcha.

For every customer who returns for a second transaction, the retailer averages $250 in sales for the next 12 months. With about 1 million new customers per year, an additional 3 percent return at an average sale of $250 results in an incremental $7.5 million of sales.

Did I hear the CFO from the back of the room, asking, "… but what did it cost you?" Let's do the math. If the 1 million postcards cost an additional 20 cents because of this new process, the additional cost would be $200,000. If there's a CFO who would not spend $200,000 for an additional $7.5 million in sales, we know a few CFO's who want his or her job.

If this principle is true, and the reduced **TLTTD** directly correlates to a higher response, why stop at the bi-weekly mailing? We could do this weekly. When my client tried exactly that, they were delighted to see an additional 1 percent increase in sales, or another $2.5 million in incremental sales. Even better, the weekly process was put into place at no additional cost. On this point, the CFO's of the world are unanimous. A sales increase of $2.5 million at no cost is a pretty good deal. In the chart below, you see the increased response rates when the normally monthly mailings were sent out on a weekly basis instead.

Month	Mailed	Resp Rate
Feb	96,970	3.43%
Mar	93,185	9.66%
Apr	92,346	8.27%
May	93,823	8.81%
Jun	94,386	9.81%

The dramatically increased response rate between February and later months occurred as mailings increased to weekly from monthly. Our enlightened retail case study, Glik's Stores, has reduced their **TLTTD** to 5–10 days. That means that the customer receives a postcard between 5 and 10 days after his or her first transaction.

My Suggestion:

> **Stand with me, put your hand on your heart, and repeat:**
>
> *We hereby hold this truth to be self-evident, that all things considered, 5–7 weeks and 5–10 days in TLTTD is not equal, and endowed as we are with technology and the wonders of First Class Mail, we will uphold our new-found <u>rights</u> to send the <u>right message</u> to the <u>right person</u> AT THE <u>RIGHT TIME</u>.*

Whether by email, voicemail, or first class mail, we will communicate with the customer as quickly as possible, not counting the costs (solely), as we believe that all strategies should be judged not by what is cheapest, but by what gets results.

We hereby pledge to do the "right" thing. And do it fast.

Have a great Independence Day!

Chapter VII

July—Money in the Mail

(Wk 1: Let's get personal)

Unless a Fourth of July full of summer "action" movies, fried food, and fireworks erased all short-term memory, you'll recall that we spent last month discussing the importance of the Customer's First Transaction. Wow. Four weeks on one little transaction?

It's not so little. After all, if the first transaction is handled correctly, we can start to build a base of loyal, profitable customers. If that first transaction is not handled correctly in the store and immediately thereafter, there will never be a second transaction—or a third. As they say in the song, the beginning is a very good place to start.

Glik Stores, our Midwest client, served as the basis for our case study on the First Customer Transaction. Glik's was a success story built gradually, piece by piece, with some suggestions from Claude Johnson Associates and plenty of trial and error on the part of Glik's. The end result was a healthy 10 percent increase for Glik's in the percentage of customers who come back for a second transaction. That translates to more than a million dollars annually in incremental sales. Clearly, this kind of increase is worth the effort of any retailer. But for a small/medium-sized company, the impact on total sales is enormous.

My mom always said, "You can't squeeze blood out of a turnip." Do you think the Johnsons were originally farmers? I wonder. Did someone ever try squeezing blood out of a turnip? I don't know. She meant that it's best to stop while you're ahead. It's not the only advice from my mother that I failed to take. Despite all good advice, there's one more thing I want to consider when it comes to the Customer's First Transaction. Conveniently, it leads us right into our message for July, which is: The Money's In The Mail. So let's squeeze that last drop of blood out of the turnip that is the Customer's First Transaction.

Can we get personal for a minute?

"Personalize: (v) to make personal or more personal. To individualize."

How personal are 100,000 mail pieces, all exactly the same except for the mailing label? Not very. Then again, we don't need to be too personal. If we can make our mail just a little *more* personal, we might still meet Webster's definition. It's only wise to move gradually towards personalization. A little goes a long way.

Let's go back to Glik's. The two direct mail pieces below were mailed in successive years, to holiday events in 2002 and 2003. If they seem similar, they should. The offer was the same, the selection criterion was the same; the length of the event was the same. The only difference is 2003's graphic.

Early on, we helped Glik's institute a thank you program for high value customers with recent large purchases. The thank you cards go out on a weekly basis with an offer designed to motivate the customer to return to the store. In 2003 this program also began to use the personalization printing capability from Kohler.

Notice the incredible results that Glik's achieved in 2003 over 2002. The chart below reflects the results for early 2002 and the annualized value of that program.

2002	Mailed	Count	Rate	Avg Spend	Total Sales
Feb	4,000	963	24.1%	$ 91.00	$ 87,615
Mar	4,000	922	23.1%	$ 88.00	$ 81,136
Apr	4,000	985	24.6%	$ 85.00	$ 83,742
Total	12,000	2,870	23.9%	$ 87.98	$252,493

2003	Mailed	Count	Rate	Avg Spend	Total Sales
Feb	4,000	1,152	28.4%	$112.00	$129,069
Mar	4,000	1,174	29.4%	$105.00	$123,312
Apr	4,000	1,095	27.4%	$ 98.00	$107,330
Total	12,000	3,422	28.5%	$105.12	$359,710

Now, experience (the one thing I've plenty of) generally shows that simply changing the graphics of a piece will have little or no impact on the response rate. Don't tell this to your graphic designer. However, the change made by Glik's was not change for change's sake. This change had a very specific purpose: to create a mail piece that was more "personal".

The personalization was accomplished by Kohler and Sons, Inc, an established printing firm in St. Louis. It is not something that most firms can do on a regular basis. Kohler has leapt into the 21st Century through the use of new technology in printing.

Kohler's technology is so useful because it allows you to be "more personal" with your customers. [The degree of personalization is left up to you and your printer, but the "more personal" without bringing privacy into play, the better. The mail pieces above are just the beginning effort by Glik's working with Kohler.] Let's look at why this is such a big deal and worth every penny of expense and effort. In the case of the two mail pieces above, the 2003 mail piece responded with 6% **more responses than the non-personalized mailing for the same event in 2002.**

Because the personalization technology is digital, each mail piece printed can have unique graphics, different verbiage, and of course different mailing labels. Can you imagine that? You build a library of different graphics, each graphic appropriate for a customer segment according to age, gender, ethnicity, geography, products purchased, etc. The graphics change "on the fly" according to the coding on the customer record being printed at that moment.

We don't need to be design experts or psychologists to see the benefit here.

Of course, Glik's paid a few dollars more for the personalization provided by Kohler. But the incremental $2,000 expense for personalization generated an incremental $428,870 in sales. That's putting the personal touch right on a customer's wallet.

How quickly are *you* going to personalize your communications?
I thought so.

Are we done here? Is there nothing else we can do for the First-Time Customer? Of course, there is. There is always room for developing new techniques and practices in retail CRM. In fact, we're going to spend the rest of the summer looking at how to make our mailings pay off—whether it's new tricks for traditional direct mail programs, or ways to adapt to the new mails: email and voice mail.

We will never get away from postal mail. It's simply not realistic to expect 100 percent capture of the email addresses or phone numbers of our customers.

We'll also never get away from the power of the personal.

My Suggestion:

> Take any small steps you can to personalize your direct mail communications.

Even with a higher production cost, the piece with the personal touch wins.

(Wk 2: All-star break)

Have you ever seen that screw-up in baseball, where two base runners end up on the same base? It's not a good thing, and one runner is automatically called out. In this *Jem*, we're going to put two base runners on the *same base* and get a *positive result*.

Don't worry, Joe Torre. We haven't changed the rules to the national pastime. We're talking direct mail pieces (the base runners) and customers (the base). We've found a new kind of double play that doesn't make outs, but brings customers in!

Recently, a client launched a direct mail campaign, with the obvious goal of driving business to the store. We selected the top one million customers out of the database to receive the mail piece. Smart direct marketers that we are, we chose the million customers based on historical responses to direct mail by monetary/recency segments. The event ran for 5 weeks, about 35 days.

	Recency Segments						
	R1 0-3 Months	**R2** 4-6 Months	**R3** 7-9 Months	**R4** 10-12 Months	**R5** 13-18 Months	**R6** 19-24 Months	**Row Total**
$ Seg	**Selected for Mailing**						
M1	36,373	7,211	2,735	1,163	1,104	446	49,033
M2	20,370	5,051	2,270	848	874	370	29,782
M3	37,475	9,950	4,739	2,184	1,908	910	57,166
M4	71,943	21,927	12,000	5,775	5,845	2,859	120,348
M5	169,781	58,644	38,020	20,263	22,810	12,456	321,974
M6	176,548	76,985	58,371	35,435	45,262	29,095	421,696
Total	**512,490**	**179,768**	**118,134**	**65,668**	**77,803**	**46,137**	**1,000,000**
	Expected Response Rate						
M1	60.8%	42.5%	28.0%	25.8%	11.7%	7.0%	**53.9%**
M2	55.1%	38.3%	27.9%	24.1%	14.6%	8.8%	**47.5%**
M3	51.3%	36.4%	25.3%	20.8%	12.9%	8.1%	**43.4%**
M4	46.0%	32.5%	23.4%	21.1%	11.3%	7.0%	**37.4%**
M5	39.3%	25.8%	18.9%	17.1%	8.8%	6.2%	**29.6%**
M6	30.6%	19.5%	14.8%	13.1%	7.2%	5.0%	**20.6%**
Total	**40.3%**	**25.5%**	**17.9%**	**15.7%**	**8.3%**	**5.5%**	**29.3%**

The chart above reflects the customer count by monetary/recency cell selected for the mailing. Below those figures, we see the expected response rate according to our historical response history. Doesn't everyone have these great response rates?

So far, so good. The mail file was then sent to the fulfillment house for printing and mailing. Sounds simple, doesn't it?

Well, as Yogi Berra would say, "it ain't over, 'till it's over." Things are rarely as simple as they seem.

A few days later, it was discovered that the fulfillment house had printed 50,000 extra pieces.

What to do? What to do?

Of course, the fulfillment house could have thrown the pieces out. Not too surprisingly, they chose instead to offer them to the client at a reduced cost, if they wanted to increase the mailing. The estimated incremental cost for the additional 50,000 was about $15,000, including postage and everything else.

Now, we had to go back into the database and pull the next best 50,000 customers. On the chart below, we can see to the right the next best 50,000 customers and their expected response rate.

	Recency Segments							R7
	R1	R2	R3	R4	R5	R6	Row	25-30
	0-3	4-6	7-9	10-12	13-18	19-24	Total	Months
	Months	Months	Months	Months	Months	Months		

$ Seg	Selected for Mailing							
M1	36,373 7,211	2,735	1,163	1,104	446		49,033	484
M2	20,370 5,051	2,270	848	874	370		29,782	401
M3	37,475 9,950	4,739	2,184	1,908	910		57,166	986
M4	71,943 21,927	12,000	5,775	5,845	2,859		120,348	3,098
M5	169,781 58,644	38,020	20,263	22,810	12,456		321,974	13,499
M6	176,548 76,985	58,371	35,435	45,262	29,095		421,696	31,532
Total	512,490 179,768	118,134	65,668	77,803	46,137		1,000,000	50,000

	Expected Response Rate							
M1	60.8%	42.5%	28.0%	25.8%	11.7%	7.0%	53.9%	4.9%
M2	55.1%	38.3%	27.9%	24.1%	14.6%	8.8%	47.5%	6.7%
M3	51.3%	36.4%	25.3%	20.8%	12.9%	8.1%	43.4%	6.0%
M4	46.0%	32.5%	23.4%	21.1%	11.3%	7.0%	37.4%	4.9%
M5	39.3%	25.8%	18.9%	17.1%	8.8%	6.2%	29.6%	4.1%
M6	30.6%	19.5%	14.8%	13.1%	7.2%	5.0%	20.6%	2.9%
Total	40.3%	25.5%	17.9%	15.7%	8.3%	5.5%	29.3%	3.4%

Some people would die for a 3.4 percent response rate. However, for this client, there was some reluctance to increase the mailing even at the reduced cost. After all, *the best we could hope for was 3.4 percent response.* In comparison, the first million customers were expected to have a 29.3 percent response rate. (We should note that the 29 percent response rate includes customers with a rate as high as 60.8 percent, all the way down to a low of 5 percent).

Faced with this dilemma, I made a rather whacko recommendation:

"Let's *remail* the top 50,000 customers, instead of mailing these next best 50,000 customers."

The client said, "Yea, what have you been drinking, Claude? Why would we waste perfectly good mail pieces by sending a customer two of them?"

I looked at the data again. Once more, I went back to the client and implored them (a nice big word for begging) to reconsider and run a test.

Selected for Re-Mailing				Expected Response Rate		
Recency Segment				Recency Segment		
R1	R2			R1	R2	
0-3 Months	4-6 Months	Row Total		0-3 Months	4-6 Months	Row Total
$				**$**		
M1 36,373	7,211	**43,584**		**M1** 60.8%	42.5%	**57.8%**
M2 20,370	5,051	**25,421**		**M2** 55.1%	38.3%	**51.7%**
M3 37,475		**37,475**		**M3** 51.3%		**51.3%**
M4		-		**M4**		
M5		-		**M5**		
M6		-		**M6**		
Total 94,218	**12,262**	**106,480**		**Total 55.8%**	**40.8%**	**54.1%**

Looking at the chart above, 54 percent of the best customers do respond to direct mail pieces, and 46 percent don't respond. Let's think about it. Do we have a better chance of getting a portion of the 46 percent of our best customers to respond than we do of getting some of the 96.6 percent (that's 100 percent - 3.4 percent) of the Next Best 50,000 who don't normally respond?

By imploring and wagering my reputation, I persuaded the client to test the concept. We took the top 106,000 customers (the customers in the 3 cells), and then randomly selected 50,000 to receive the second mailing. We kept the other 56,000 as a control group, to receive only the one mailing.

We measured the sales for both groups, from the time of receipt of the second mail piece to the end of the event. The remail went out about two weeks into the event.

Guess what happened?

Incremental Sales Calculation for March, 2006 Catalog Remail Test

	Mailed	Control	Incremental Resp Rate	Cust Count
Cust Cnt	50,000	50,000		
Resp	20,971	19,429		
1-Resp Rate	41.94%	38.86%	3.08%	1,542
Sales	$ 4,913,352	$ 4,438,540		
2-Avg Spend	$ 234.29	$ 228.45	$ 5.84	

Incremental Sales due to
1-Resp Rate	$ 361,279
2-Avg Spend	$ 113,532
Total	**$ 474,811**

The remail group generated over $450,000 in incremental sales, compared to the control group during the same time frame. Our cost was about $15,000. Had the cost been fully loaded (that's with no mistake by the fulfillment house), it would have run us about $25,000.

What did we learn?

Most importantly, we proved that sometimes whacko ideas can work in retail. We should take advantage of other's mistakes, especially if it doesn't cost us anything. Let's test ideas before rolling them out.

My Suggestion:

> **Don't remail all customers, but test until you find the breakeven recency/ monetary cells.**

Then stop. I wouldn't recommend that you remail every mailing. Customers will get irritated at all those trees being wasted.

But if we've got our strategy right, we can put two men on the same base, and score big time. As crazy as it sounds, remailing a reminder can work.

As Yogi would say, it'll be "déjà vu, all over again …"

(Wk 3: Value in statistics)

Having drawn one baseball analogy last week, it got me thinking a little more about the Grand Old Game, and what we can learn from it. As any grizzled baseball man can tell us, while he pours through yesterday's box scores and scouting reports, baseball is a game of numbers: batting averages, ERA's, and RBI's. "If ya wanna talk baseball, ya gotta know yer stats." The Grand Old Game of retail CRM is no different. If we want to maximize our mailing efforts, we better break down the numbers, and take a look at our results.

Of course, it's always more fun to dissect a win than a loss. So let's take a look at a recent marketing event that worked, and see what really led to the victory. This particular direct mail event was for Friday, Saturday, and Sunday after Thanksgiving, a period when all retailers are competing for face-time and customer sales. It was pressure time: bases loaded, tie game, bottom of the ninth, with two outs. How did we do? The chart below represents our box score:

	Mailed File	Control File	Incremental
Mailed	100,350	7,520	
Responders	13,521	660	
Resp Rate	13.5%	8.8%	4.7%
Total Sales	$850,409	$45,605	
Avg Trans	$62.90	$69.11	($6.22)

The first thing to notice is that this retailer did the right thing: they kept out a control file of 7,250 customers who did not receive the mailer. Those customers were tracked during the event. CFOs love these control file analysis, and well they should. This file is what allows us to see our real results.

For example, in looking at the figures above, we can see that 8.8 percent of the control list came to the store and purchased during the sales event. They are called "walk ins." In fact, they had an average transaction that was $6.22 higher than the mailed file. If we take credit for those sales, we're skewing our numbers for the event. Those customers never received the postcard, so they certainly couldn't have been influenced by it.

On the other hand, the mailed file (those receiving the postcard), responded at a rate of 13.5 percent, with an average transaction of $62.90. The reason this group had a lower amount than the control file for the average transaction was that those in the mailed group were making their purchases at a discount. They had received a private discount offer, not available to the control file shoppers.

All in all, the stats for the event look pretty impressive. Most companies would be pleased with a response anywhere close to this. Still, before we tip our cap to the crowd, let's take an in-depth look at our results. How good were they?

In this game of direct mail, the score is measured in incremental sales:

Incremental Sales Due to <u>Response Rate</u>

Incremental Response Rate	4.7%
Incremental Transactions	4,715
Average Transaction	$62.90
Inc. Sales	$296,575

Incremental Sales Due to <u>Average Transaction</u>

Average Transaction	($6.22)
Response Rate	8.8%
Transactions	8,805
Inc. Sales	$ (54,740)
Total Incremental Sales	$241,835
Cost	$ 36,000

Incremental sales are driven by two separate, but important, aspects of mailing. First, incremental sales are determined by the lift, or the incremental Response Rate. Since those who received the postcard responded at a much higher rate than those who did not receive the postcard, this event generated a very large incremental sales number ($296,575).

Second, incremental sales are related to the incremental Average Transaction. Typically, we will find a positive number for the incremental average transaction. But in this case, the average transaction declined, due to the strength of the discount offer for those who received the postcard. The moral of the story is: You have to take the bad with the good. Since the average transaction went down, the incremental sales number related to this factor was negative (-$54,740).

Nevertheless, when we add up the scorecard, it's pretty clear we have a victory in the making. The total of the incremental Response Rate and the incremental Average Transaction shows total incremental sales of $241,835. Even when we factor in costs of $36,000 for creative, printing, mailing services and postage, we're looking pretty good. Would you spend $36,000 to get incremental sales of $241,835?

I have yet to meet the retail CFO who wouldn't spend a buck to get six back in incremental sales.

Call that one a home run. Yet, the real education is in looking at some of the smaller segments in the mailing, to see how they responded in comparison to other segments. Happily, the marketing staff for this retailer learned from an old sage who said: "If you can't measure it, you can't change it." They measure everything.

There's one more wrinkle that we haven't yet discussed. It wasn't just direct mail driving this event. Like that fireball-throwing closer coming out of the bullpen, we had a secret weapon that helped seal this particular victory. The analysis so far has been for customers who received the traditional postcard. But the retailer also tested the use of a relatively new technology: voice messaging.

Okay. I know. The first response is: "I hate telemarketers". This is not like your father's Oldsmobile. It's warm and fuzzy (the message, not the Oldsmobile), like all our communications with customers should be. Better yet, it allowed us to cut through the clutter of our competition, to connect directly with our customer.

Keep in mind that this particular selling event was a Thanksgiving promotion. It's not exactly a unique idea in retailing. How do we separate ourselves from all those other stores filling our customers' mailboxes, advertising in their newspapers, and knocking on their doors? One way—maybe the best way—is to actually *speak* to our customer.

That can be easier said than done.

Do we get all store personnel to gather around and start dialing for dollars, calling every customer on the database? **Noooo.**

Do we offer a 12-Step program to associates afraid to call customers? **Noooo.**

Do we have associates, many of whom can't be understood, leave strange and confusing solicitations on the customers' answering machines? **Noooo.**

Do we ask our friendly CFO to fund the payroll for this fiasco? **Noooo.**

What did we do? It's simple. We called our friends at Smart Reply, a professional voice mail service provider.

We spent a few hours with Smart Reply, talking about the event, our goals, and the number of customers to be called. Together, we designed the script, approved it all, and promptly got out of the way to let the pros handle the project. Let's check that scorecard one more time:

Cust Segment	Post cards only		Postcard and Phone		Incremental	
	Resp Rate	Avg Trans	Resp Rate	Avg Trans	Resp Rate	Avg Trans
1Responders	16.8%	$52.50	22.81%	$ 56.31	5.97%	$ 3.82
2Best Cust.	12.3%	$65.85	18.37%	$ 72.48	6.10%	$ 6.63
3New Stores	13.8%	$52.57	15.94%	$ 66.81	2.10%	$ 14.23
4Other	15.9%	$69.63	20.64%	$ 64.09	4.75%	$ (5.54)
Total Mailing	13.5%	$62.90	19.36%	$ 68.11	5.89%	$ 5.21

1) **Total lift** was an incremental 5.89 percent response rate and a $5.21 incremental average transaction. This is the best of both worlds: more responses and larger expenditures.

2) **Incremental lift** was across all 4 customer segments. Trust Barry Bonds on this: bigger is better. I'm talking about the size of the lift of phone contacts, versus contacts via direct mail.

3) **Responders**—We've discovered that responders from previous direct mail events will continue responding at a very high rate.

4) **Best Customers**—Self-explanatory.

5) **New Stores**—We wanted to see how new store customers might respond differently.

6) **Other**—I always like other segments. I was Vice President of Other at NBO Menswear in the early 90's: whatever no one wanted, I got. The same thing

happens here. If they don't belong to the segments above, they are "other." Even "other" was successful.

Just like baseball, CRM takes a little teamwork. By itself, voice messaging might not generate big sales. But used in concert with our other CRM techniques, it has a terrific synergistic effect on the results for a promotional event.

My Suggestion:

   Play the numbers.

Use statistics to learn how to maximize your results. And don't neglect the secret weapon—a voice mail message that speaks to your customer!

(Wk 4: Statistics—the human side)

My father used to say, "Son, you don't know what you don't know." Last week, we talked about the value of statistics when it comes to maximizing our results from CRM initiatives. However, there's a danger to statistics as well. It may be true that numbers don't lie, but insufficient analysis does. If we're looking at the numbers to understand our results, then we'd better not rely solely on what we know. We'd better try to find out what we don't know.

From the chart below, you will see the statistics for a normal, every day direct mail event: 100,000 pieces mailed, 5 percent response, and a $125,000 gross margin generated on the event. Looking at this data, most of us would chalk it up as a successful event and leave it at that. But if we're using these numbers to measure our results and to make future decisions, we might want to go a little deeper. Make sure the results are valid.

Example

A

100,000	Quantity Mailed
5.0%	Response Rate
5,000	Transactions
$50.00	Average Transaction Dollars
$250,000	Sales Generated from the Event
$125,000	Gross Margin Dollars (assume 50%)
$60,000	Cost of the Event

What really happened with this event? Are there some things we don't know?

Plenty!

Let's start with the average transaction. Was it really more or less than the number in the chart? This depends on which portion of the customers we captured as responders. Obviously, if we captured only the small transaction responders and not all responders, the average transaction would be deflated. If we captured primarily the large transaction responders, the average would be inflated. What really happened?

To measure the success or failure of an event is fairly simple. All we have to do is keep track of those who receive the communication (postal, email or voice messaging), then see if any of those customers purchase during the time frame of the event. Those are our respondents.

Therein lies the rub. As far as our measurement facility is concerned, a customer is only identified as a respondent if the transaction is coded with some sort of customer identifier. That identifier (a customer number, loyalty card number, telephone number, credit card number or email address) will alert the measurement facility to the fact that this customer was part of the promotion and thus they are measured as a respondent. *If there is no customer identifier on the transaction, or the customer identifier is not part of the mail list,* then this customer will not be considered a respondent to the direct mail program. It's simple as pie.

What if our store's process, and our capture of customer information, is a little less than perfect? What?! In retail? Say it ain't so, Joe. When it comes to capturing customer information, I've yet to see a perfect process or infallible execution. Imagine …

Cue: Scary music. Through the mist, we watch Dream Sequence #1:

The customer comes in, responding to the direct mail offering. Unfortunately, at the point of purchase, the associate is not diligent in matching up this customer to his or her previous customer record. Instead, the associate decides it would be easier to create a new customer record. Hello new customer—goodbye, respondent. This customer will never be measured as a respondent to the direct mail piece, as he or she now has a different customer number and the new customer number is not on the mailed file.

As one customer disappears into a vapor, a new one emerges, for Dream Sequence #2:

The customer responds to the direct mail piece by making a purchase, which the sales associate properly attributes to the customer's number. But alas! There are duplicate records in our customer database! I know no one reading this has ever experienced it, but some retailers actually have duplicate records on their database. If the customer record selected for the mailing is not the same one to which the sale is credited, we've just lost another respondent.

Yikes. It gives me the shivers, just thinking about it.

"All right, all right, Claude" the retailers refrain. "Why is there so much focus on the negative? The event was successful. Let's accentuate the positive!" Yes, indeed. The only problem is that future decisions will be made based on the data. More often than not, wrong data = wrong decisions. It's all about knowing what we don't know.

Purely as an academic exercise, I selected two different clients, and attempted to find out if there were in fact some customers who received a mail piece and responded, but were not properly measured. So I pulled all transactions during a selected promotional event that had customer information, but did not have a customer number that matched the list of customers mailed. In other words, these were customers, but not respondents.

Then, I proceeded to run those transactions through a de-duping processing (also known as merge/purge). With a little effort, I was able to match these customer purchases to a matching name on the mail list. So these were respondents, after all.

"Big deal," the retailers sighed. "Of course, there are always a few bad apples." In both cases, it was only about one percent of the mail file. Still, just for argument's sake, let's transpose that to our initial case study. For the 100,000 mailed, these mistakes would have excluded an additional 1000 responders, $50,000 in sales, or $25,000 in Gross Margin Dollars. For a new CRM convert, this might have helped make the decision whether to continue using direct mail.

Example

A	B	
100,000	100,000	Quantity Mailed
5.0%	4.0%	Response Rate
5,000	4,000	Transactions
$50.00	$50.00	Average Transaction Dollars
$250,000	$200,000	Sales Generated from the Event
$125,000	$100,000	Gross Margin Dollars (assume 50%)
$60,000	$60,000	Cost of the Event

In the chart, Example (B) reflects what the measured results in this case study would have been, had the retailer not captured accurate data at the point of sale. Things begin to look a little gray and fuzzy. Would we spend $60,000 to generate

$100,000 in gross margin? Hmm. Maybe, unless we could find something better in which to invest.

It's enough to leave a dedicated CRM guy tossing and turning in his bed, vexed by all that he doesn't know. Consider this one:

There's that scary music again ...

The customer responds to the mail piece by making a purchase, but the sales associate is (a) new (b) untrained (c) asleep at the wheel and fails to identify the customer at all. Needless to say, the customer is a respondent but is never measured.

Example

A	B	C	
100,000	100,000	100,000	Quantity Mailed
5.0%	4.0%	3.0%	Response Rate
5,000	4,000	3,000	Transactions
$50.00	$50.00	$50.00	Average Transaction Dollars
$250,000	$200,000	$150,000	Sales Generated from the Event
$125,000	$100,000	$75,000	Gross Margin Dollars (assume 50%)
$60,000	$60,000	$60,000	Cost of the Event

Ouch. This hurts. It hurts because there's no way to determine the extent of this particular problem. My 20-year experience in retail would suggest that it's at least as common as the inaccurate capture of data. If inaccurate capture accounts for a one percent reduction in our case-study results, then non-capture would certainly lower our response rate by another percent. Now, we're looking at a three percent response rate, a $75,000 gross margin generated for $60,000 in costs. Would anyone put their neck on the line for results like this?

My Suggestion:

   Don't settle for what you know, or think you know.

Dig deeper, and find out what you don't know. CRM decisions are only as good as the numbers on which they're based.

All of our errors in database management and customer capture come back to haunt us, by diminishing our results and misleading us in our analysis. We have to pay as much attention to capturing customer information as we do to capturing financial information.

Whoever said "What you don't know won't hurt you," was never in retail CRM.

Chapter VIII

August — Money in the New Mail

(Wk 1: Reruns, pilots, hit shows)

Is it hot enough for you?

Welcome to the dog days of summer. And it's not always the heat that really gets to you. No—not the humidity either. It's the reruns.

'Tis the season of nothing but the same old television shows, interspersed with extravagant advertisements for all the great stuff coming in the fall. So we sit, slaves to the air-conditioning and a cable box with one hundred channels and nothing to watch.

That's at home, of course. At work, we have a whole different set of channels—and all of them are worth looking at. It won't surprise you then that this month, we're going to do exactly that.

In July, we looked at the money in the mail—the good old traditional mail, that is. No doubt about it, direct mail continues to be our primary means of communication to the customer. Some things are slow to change.

Other things are not. Back in the old days (thankfully, my career did not precede the invention of regular mail, but I've seen the invention of most other technologies) there were far fewer communication channels available to a retailer. By now, even the dinosaurs among us have caught up with at least some of the new technologies out there, whether it's email, or voicemail.

Still, do we understand these new technologies well enough to make intelligent decisions about which one to use, and when? The money's in the mail, all right—new and old. But if we want to design an effective customer campaign, our task is to choose the right channel, at the right time. Even better, we can combine the right channels in a perfectly synchronized approach.

Back in those golden days before the advent of email and voicemail messaging, I remember working with the Vice President of Stores for a menswear retailer. We ran a test, using a group of customers for whom we had telephone numbers in our database. Each customer received a call from a sales associate at the same time that he or she received a postcard reminder about an upcoming sales event. We discovered that customers who got the call had an incremental response rate 2.5 percent higher than those customers who were not called. In addition, the average transaction for the called group was $25 more than the non-called group.

Some things don't change. As has been noted over and over again in direct marketing journals, the more channels of communication that we use to contact the customer, the higher the response rate we can expect. Today, our options for mixing and matching are greatly expanded.

A client just completed a direct mail campaign, announcing a sale event. In the past, we would have sent a simple postcard to the selected customers. But we discovered that the client's database included some very valuable data: email addresses and telephone numbers. In some cases, the company had both email address and telephone number.

We wanted to know which channel would be the most effective way to inform the selected customers of the upcoming sales event. Being the CRM scientists that we are, we ran a test, pitting the postcard against email, voice messaging, and the combination of both email and voice messaging.

Once again, some things don't change. Among the various channels, the old reliable postcard was still the winner in total purchases. How did it fare against telephone and email or both?

Of the 673,000 customers selected, 10 percent of the records had an email address, 9 percent had a telephone number, and 5.5 percent of the records had both email and telephone information. Do you know what percent of your file has email addresses and phone numbers? The chart below reflects the counts for each status:

Customer Count	Segment
506,000	Segment 1-Postcard-No email-No phone
67,000	Segment 2-Postcard + Email
63,000	Segment 3-Postcard + Voice Message
37,000	Segment 4-Postcard + Email + Voice Message
673,000	**Total Selected Customers**

When the event was over, Segment 1 (postcard only) generated a 6 percent incremental response over the control group, and $4,200,000 in incremental sales over control. Not bad, eh? The other three segments had incremental response rates over control of 7.6, 7.0 and 8.3 percent, respectively. The three segments together generated over $360,000 in incremental sales over control. It seems small compared to $4,200,000 from the postcard only segment. You might say, "It wasn't worth all the trouble." Not so fast, Mikey.

When we look at the Return on Investment for the new communications channels, we get a very different perspective. The weighted cost of these communications was $.02 for email, $.08 for voice messaging, and $.10 for both.

Why would we spend ten cents to communicate to a customer, if we can simply email them for two cents? Three letters: R-O-I. We do it because we get a 214 percent return on investment.

Here are a couple more reasons to consider the new mail, along with old:

- Less pain, for the gain. It's much easier to prepare email or voice message communication than a printed piece, given the cost of printing, color proofing, and graphics.

- We're talking "turnaround". Direct mail can take a few days to a few weeks to develop and deliver to the customer, compared to email, which can happen in only a few hours. Voice messaging takes a little bit longer, usually from 24 to 48 hours. A quicker turnaround means that we can include very recent transactions in our selection—a feature that vastly increases the relevance of our message and also increases the response rate.

- Pennies Pay. Email can be as little as half a penny to 1.5 pennies per email and voice messaging can be as little as 6 to 10 pennies, depending upon volume. That's a pretty substantial savings over the Postal Service.

Don't get me wrong. I am still the staunchest proponent of a good direct mail marketing program. The more things change, the more that particular thing remains the same. Still, why not use all of the technological tools we have available? If the ROI is right, then we should **communicate** any way we can.

My Suggestion:

Keep your eyes open to any and all of the new mail options, and be prepared to use them.

Remember, these case studies were only possible because the companies had the customer information they needed. Institute programs and procedures for acquiring email addresses and telephone numbers for your customers.

If we get bored watching the same old shows again and again, imagine how our customer feels. Let's find the right channel, and show 'em something new once in a while. This month, we'll look at our options, and find the money in the new mail!

(Wk 2: The e-mail hour—what a show!)

Who isn't looking for a "new" solution? Admit it. We love our *new* technology, *new and improved* products, *new* solutions, and the latest fashion—we're retailers, after all. Hope springs eternal with each new invention. Now, at last, we will be able to do what we were never able to do before. In fact, we'll do it better, cheaper, and faster—all thanks to the *new*.

Then reality sets in. It's not so much that the new thing doesn't work as advertised. Often, it really is better, cheaper, and faster. If only …

Life would be so much better if only we could rid ourselves of those same old Achilles Heels that have always tripped us up in the past. Unfortunately, our lack of follow-through, our inattention to detail, and our office politics screw up the new solutions, just like they did our old solutions. It's not the new tricks that stymie the old dogs. It's those old habits that can't be broken.

Take the *new* solution of email communication, for example. What an invention! Email messaging offers us the fastest, often the most responsive, and definitely the least expensive method of communicating to our customer. With this technology, it costs almost nothing to communicate, assuming that we have taken the essential step of acquiring our customers' email addresses.

Oh.…

Here's where the new solution crashes into the same old problem: the difficulty of identifying the customer at the point of sale. Now, it's no longer sufficient to identify the home address of the customer. We also need the email address. If we're going to take that giant leap into the future, we're first going to have to solve the problems of the past. How do we acquire the customer's email address?

1. If we prefer an old fashioned solution, we could just ask. Of course, this is easier said than done. Do we really want to hold up the sales transaction to get an email address, assuming the customer is willing to give it? How accurate will that address be, if the sales clerk who enters it at the Point of Sale (POS) is in a rush to complete the transaction?

    While a misspelled home address can still be delivered by our faithful mail carrier, one incorrect character in an email address will result in a bounce. Have you seen some of those cute email names and complicated domain names?

2. We can ask the customer to fill out a form with the email address, and enter it into the customer database. I have a client who is running a sweepstakes, in which the customer is invited to drop his or her name, address and email address in a "fish bowl" to win 50,000 air miles. Hopefully, all the customer forms are legible and the data entry clerks are accurate.

3. If we have a web page, we can direct customers to the website, and solicit his or her email address on the site. I have another client who is using their loyalty program to give customers bonus points for providing an email address. Believe me; the cost of those points is miniscule compared to the benefit of acquiring the information.

4. If we actually sell on the web, we can probably acquire the email address as a part of each transaction. We'll need this information in order to provide the customer with updates on the status of their order.

Here's an even easier way to get the customer's email address—and it's likely to sound familiar: email appending from a third party data provider. This works in much the same way as the reverse telephone append, which we discussed several months ago. If we have the customer's mailing address, we can send this information to a third party and receive back the customer's email address.

All of you privacy advocates out there don't panic. When a third party provider matches an email address to our customer file, they will send the customer an email, asking if he or she would like to receive messages from the retailer, and giving the customer an opt-out alternative. On top of that, every retailer I know offers the customer an opt-out in each subsequent email communication.

Some third parties maintain their own email list and some broker several lists. Depending on the size and demographics of these lists in comparison to the demographics of our customer file, we can usually expect a match rate of 10–20 percent. Since no list provider has all the email addresses in the world, brokers will normally match against multiple lists to increase the number of matches. All of this can be done in less than a couple of weeks, at a cost between 20–50 cents per email address (the cost is for each address returned to the retailer.)

Great, isn't it? Now that we've figured out how to get all those email addresses, just imagine all we can do with them …

"Do? Did you say 'do something'?" Oooh. There's another old problem, rearing its ugly head.

One could assume that there would be a plan for how to use the email addresses after acquisition. Instead, the whole issue often becomes a hot potato, passed as quickly as possible on to someone else. "We've never done anything like this before. What if we try something and it goes wrong?"

Sound familiar? See if this story strikes a chord:

Here's a company that sold through all three channels: retail, catalog and web. Using their points-based loyalty program, the company decided to reward top customers with a 4-day, double-points event. This was to be promoted through a postcard to 50,000 customers. Simple?

Yea, right. Since the event was intended primarily to drive retail traffic, the catalog and web group immediately divorced themselves from the program. "You're on your own," was heard in the halls. But of course, this was hardly unexpected, as the divisions had never cooperated in the past on any information sharing.

When asked if a reminder message to the customers could be sent via email, the web group stalled, with a laundry list of concerns:

1. we need a web designer to design the message

2. it will take too long

3. we have never done this

4. those email addresses are ours (are there really organizations that have silos of information that are "owned" by one channel? Methinks so.)

5. the email addresses aren't valid

6. someone will be needed to answer all the customer questions

Is that enough to give you the flavor of the CRM environment at this company? Fortunately, the IT department did not answer to any one of the channels of distribution. Consequently, the email addresses were made available (7,000 of the 50,000 top tier customers), and a reminder message was developed and sent out on the night before the event began. Total cost: Nothing. Zip, zots, zero.

What did the company get for its trouble? The 43,000 customers who received only the postcard responded at a 6 percent rate, while the 7,000 who got the email reminder as well as the postcard responded at 8 percent. Since the average transaction was $125, that amounted to an additional $125,000, for no incremental cost. My mother used to say, "You never get something for nothing." This was the first time in my life that I managed to get something for nothing, without my mother yelling at me.

Having vanquished all doubters with these results, surely rejoicing rang through the halls of the organization. Well, not exactly. Actually, the web group was offended by the use of their email addresses and built walls to prevent any such future use. In response, the retail channel began an effort to acquire the email address for "their customers" in the stores, with no plans to share the information with web or catalog.

YOU MIGHT THINK THIS IS FICTION. IT IS NOT. IT ACTUALLY HAPPENED.

Consider what might have happened, if the organizations were working together. Here's where we get into the science fiction!

1. There would not be 3 silos of customer data. It would all be on one customer database, with all channels having access to the data for their own uses.

2. When the event was decided upon, all channels would have been involved in making the customer's experience as easy as possible, and of maximum benefit to the company.

3. The customer care center would have been involved to the extent necessary to prepare for the increase of customer questions.

4. The email message would give the customer the option to purchase in any channel, with links to the proper web page for online purchase or information about the nearest bricks and mortar location.

5. The effort to acquire email addresses would have begun months in advance, across all 3 channels. To have email addresses for only 14 percent (7,000 of 50,000) of top tier customers is sinful.

If we could make that science-fiction scenario a reality, there's a whole array of opportunities we could address:

•   Since customers in the loyalty program get special offers on their birthday, an electronic birthday card could be sent reminding them of their birthday offering.

- When customers in the loyalty program get special offers during the year, the reminder messages could be sent much closer to the time of the offers.

- If new merchandise arrives which might be appropriate for the targeted customer (or which the customer has requested), a new arrival message could be sent.

- When something special is going on in the store or mall, messages could be sent to customers in the store's market area.

- If store hours change (to holiday hours, for instance), customers could be informed.

- If construction or remodeling is happening, an announcement could be made.

- When services are complete (alterations, special orders from another location), customers could be notified.

My Suggestion:

> Embrace the new—especially new technologies like email messaging, which offer your organization such a high ROI.

At the same time, face up to the old—the old problems, that is. Fix the problems of information-gathering and information-sharing, to make sure that you get the full benefits of this brave new world of customer communication!

(Wk 3: Simply the BEST [redux])

Okay, here's the scenario:

It's Monday morning, and we've dutifully gathered at the President's Management Meeting. The conversation turns to last week's dismal sales performance. The President is fuming. What's being done? How are we going to make sure that this week isn't another repeat of last week's results? Where are the solutions?

The President wants to:

1) get sales back where they belong (there's a Board of Directors meeting next week)
2) recover sales we might have lost due to the hurricane, or
3) screw around with our minds.

He has an idea. (Thank goodness. Does he have to do everything around here?). He suggests that each store call their best customers and invite them into the store this weekend.

Does he have any sense of the effort required to do this? Of course not. He is the President.

However, he does have the full backing of the entire executive staff, who assures him that this is a fine plan—an excellent use of that valuable customer database and a worthwhile endeavor for the sales associates. There are pats on the back as the meeting disburses, with one and all convinced that sales will soon be back on track.

Then what?

After a frenzied morning of phone calls to the store managers, it is discovered that none of the store personnel actually know who their best customers are. This means that someone will have to create a list for each store. That responsibility will fall on the Manager of the Customer Database.

Confident in the assumption that everyone will agree with his definition of the "best customers", the Manager of the Database jumps right into the project. He selects the top 200 customers for each store—assuming a hundred stores, that's a list of 20,000 customers. By Wednesday morning, he has sent the list to the stores—encouraging (no, commanding) the sales associates to call each customer and invite him or her into the store this weekend.

Of course, this goal will require that all calls be completed before Friday. If each call takes about 3–5 minutes for the sales associate, our sellers will be spending about 600 minutes reaching out to the 200 top customers in each location. This is about 10 man-hours per store.

Luckily, the sales associates have nothing to do anyway, so they are able to complete all the calls on Thursday. They record who was contacted and update the customer database, in order to track results. By Friday, the stores report back to the home office: "Mission Accomplished!"

Naturally, weekend sales are terrific. Next week's Monday morning meeting is full of congratulations for the entire executive staff. "Job well done," declares the President, hurrying off to the Board of Directors meeting. "Next time, let's try it with a larger group of customers!"

Fat chance. Let's hit rewind, and see what really happened …

Since the definition of "best customer" is left to the Database Manager, he pulls the list of largest purchasers, regardless of when their last purchase was. (Lifetime purchases are his favorite metric). As this is a store event, he doesn't include catalog and web purchases. He has no idea if the telephone numbers are not correct, nor does he look for duplicate telephone numbers across this 20,000 customer list. He simply prints a report of the best customers, in no particular sequence, and sends it in an envelope to the stores. The instructions in the envelope say: "Call these people and get them in the store this weekend".

The envelope arrives at the stores on Thursday. It takes the Store Manager 3 hours to divvy up the list to the sales associates that are on duty that day. This process is made even more difficult by the fact that the sequence of the listing has no relationship to sales associates in the store. The on-duty associates decide not to call the customers of off-duty associates, under the hallowed principle of "not my customer." The associates do call a couple of customers, but because the associates have received no training to develop phone skills, they have nothing to say to the people they call. Realizing that they are missing valuable selling time (they are on commission after all), they soon stop calling all together.

Nevertheless, the sales staff tells the Store Manager, "All calls made". This is quickly relayed to the home office. Imagine the surprise when sales for the weekend are even worse than before. This could be because the calls weren't actually made. Duh.

At next Monday's meeting, the CFO can't help asking, "What did this fiasco cost us anyway?"

Assuming 100 stores, 200 customers or 20,000 calls, at 3 minutes per call, we can figure on about 60,000 minutes or 1,000 man-hours.

1. Payroll cost is about $10,000 to $20,000
2. Don't even think about the telephone charges
3. But do consider the sales lost while the associates are not on the floor selling. If we average $100 sales per man-hour, that's $100,000 in lost sales. Maybe it's a good thing the associates never made the calls.

The actual cost could easily be $50,000 to $100,000. Some retailers do this quarterly or even monthly. The annual cost can be several hundreds of thousands of dollars with no real way of measuring the impact.

And don't forget about the hidden costs. What was the quality of those calls? Did they present the desired image to our top customers? Do the associates all speak English clearly? Could they be understood? Was the message correct? It's quite possible that the long-term damage outweighed the short-term benefit accrued.

Maybe next time the President should read "*Jems from Johnsons*" before he announces his new idea.

If he did, he'd already know about our friends at Smart Reply. This whole exercise could have been easily executed by a reputable voice messaging company. Here are two better and brighter scenarios:

Scenario One: Everything is outsourced to Smart Reply.

They record the desired message; we approve it; a list of the customers and telephone numbers is sent to Smart Reply and the calls are made. We then receive records showing which numbers were contacted, so that we can easily measure the results. From beginning to end, the process could take from 1–3 days. We know the calling was done; we know who was contacted; and we can measure the effect of the calling on the customers' purchase patterns.

Scenario 2: Only the calling is outsourced.

Smart Reply calls this their "ASP Solution." Assuming we have someone in our organization who sounds like the nicest customer service representative in the world (or at least he or she sounds human), we can record our own messages, test and approve the script, and release the calling by sending the phone list to Smart Reply. We control the entire project.

We even have the capability to personalize the message. Perhaps we want to vary the message for different regions of the country, or different stores. All we need to do is record separate messages, break out the total calling list by whatever criteria we desire, and submit the information to Smart Reply. These personalized messages will generate greater results, at little or no cost.

That's enough of the hypothetical scenarios. Let's look at a real-life case study:

The marketing event highlighted below was a back to school promotion, much like the ones almost every retailer in the country is running right now. There was a bit of a rush to get a mail piece out, as the retailer wanted to be part of the initial timing for the BTS rush. Can it get any better than sending out a mail piece and seeing immediate results?

The mailing quantity of 80,000 resulted in 3.74 percent response in the first 2 weeks, with $164,175 in sales attributable to the mail piece. The average customer spent $54.91 versus the normal average of $43.00. Not bad, right? But it wasn't just the mail piece that did it.

Since I had gone out on a limb to recommend using that newfangled mail technology, voice messaging, I thought it a good idea to measure the results.

The chart below reflects only the first 2 weeks results even though the overall results were just described.

Customers Contacted	Resp	Resp Rate	Sales	Avg Spend	Channel of Communication
27,760	1,190	4.29%	$ 71,964	$60.47	Voice Messaging
14,290	680	4.76%	$ 32,945	$48.45	Live Answer
37,950	1,120	2.95%	$ 59,267	$52.92	Postcard Only
80,000	2,990	3.74%	$164,175	$54.91	Grand Total

The voice message was delivered in two different ways:

1. **Live answer**—A person picked up the phone and answered. This happened 14,290 times. In this case, a very short, recorded message was left.

   I know we've all had those recorded messages. Give it a chance. This message begins by saying "This is … from … company and this is a recorded message." It turns out that a customer who has a relationship with the company will tend to wait and listen. The customers who received the live answer message responded at a rate of 4.76%, or about 50% more than the postcard only segment.

2. **Voice message**—No one answered the phone, but the computer detected an answering machine and a short voice message was left. This happened 27,760 times. Again, the response rate was almost twice that for those who received only the direct mail piece. Even better, there was a marked increase in the average spend of about 50% over the postcard only segment.

Don't get me wrong on this. I do not diminish the value of clientele calls from store personnel to customers with whom they have a relationship. But let's be realistic. We can't expect every customer to be called for every event by every salesperson.

My Suggestion:

Work hand-in-hand with store personnel to help you identify those customers who should have the personal touch of a live person making the call.

Then, contact the balance of customers with a warm, fuzzy, soft voice messaging call. It's (1) inexpensive (2) responsive (3) measurable (4) quick to execute. Oh, and one more thing: the results are staggering.

(Wk 4: Text messaging—"NWS 2 U")

The problem with invention is that it just doesn't stop. One new technology shows up and immediately requires another new technology to take advantage of it—you can't have mp3's without iPods. To the young among us, this is known as progress. To the rest of us, it means that no sooner have we learned one new skill than we are called upon to master another.

Several years ago, I noticed a little envelope in the corner of my cell phone screen, indicating that I had a message waiting. Rapid response, ever-ready consultant that I am, I immediately dialed my voicemail. Must be another high-ranking retail executive calling, desperate for my counsel …

Except … there was nothing there. "You have no new messages," I was told. I checked again. Nothing. Still, that tiny envelope wouldn't go away. Days later, the envelope was there, looming on my cell phone screen, as ominous as a letter from the IRS in the mailbox. No matter what I tried, there was no way to find the message, open it, or respond to it. And yet, it wouldn't go away.

Desperate, I finally turned to the solution of last resort. I read the instruction book to my cell phone. This is how I learned about text messaging.

That mysterious little envelope at the top of my screen had indeed been trying to tell me that I had a message. But it wasn't a voicemail message. I had a new kind of communication—less obtrusive than a cell phone call, shorter and more immediate than an email. Once I recovered from the embarrassment of belatedly discovering a technology that the rest of my family had been using for a year, I had to acknowledge that here was another great opportunity to communicate.

Last week, we tracked a voice messaging campaign, in which 42,050 contacts were made. Our communication play had three variables:

(1) If the call received a live answer, a recorded message was left.

(2) If the call reached an answering machine, a recorded message was left.

(3) If the phone number was a cell phone, no call was made and no message left.

It's like I said before. Every new technology brings a new benefit, and a new challenge. Clearly, one of the primary benefits of the cell phone is the ability to reach people anytime, anywhere. Naturally, there is a very high live answer rate with cell phones, because the consumers are carrying their phones with them.

The challenge is: no one wants to receive a pre-recorded message anytime, anywhere. We don't need to ask the recipient of the call "Is this a bad time?" If it's a pre-recorded message to a cell phone, it's always a bad time.

Still, it's a shame to let all those customers for whom we only have a cell phone number go without a reminder about our upcoming store event, especially after we've seen the results that such a reminder can generate. If only we had a kinder, gentler way to reach out to these customers. Maybe a new technology …

In last week's case study, there were 6,000 customers with a cell phone who were not reminded of the offer for which they had received a postcard. Judging from the success we had with customers who did receive the reminder, this inability to communicate with the cell phone users cost us $4,800 in sales. It also cost a segment of our customers the opportunity to take advantage of the offer.

Like any warm-blooded retailer, I hate to leave money on the table. In this instance, it was only 6,000 customers. What if we were working with a larger customer population? Instead of 6,000 customers, what if we were talking about 500,000 customers? It's a problem worth a call to our friends at Smart Reply.

Happily, the folks at Smart Reply are not still puzzling about the meaning of the little envelope on their phone. They are already in the text messaging business, having recognized a good opportunity when they saw it. How many people actually use text messaging? Take a look:

      18–24 years----75%

      25–34 years----48%

      35–44 years----37%

      45–54 years----21%

      55+--------------14%

I take some solace in the fact that my age group is not even on the chart. I guess most of us are still using smoke signals. But certainly, as time goes on, more of us will use text messaging—just as soon as we acquire this new fangled invention called the cell phone.

Working with Smart Reply and a very large retailer (over 5000 stores), we identified that about 25 percent of the customers were not being contacted during marketing events because their contact was a cell phone. This retailer has a younger than normal population, which not only raised the portion of customers in this non-contact group, but increased the urgency for a solution. In many cases, traditional communications like direct mail, voice messaging, and newspaper advertisements fail to reach this young consumer.

A Claude"ism": The more a customer segment is left out of the communication strategy, the more this customer segment will respond when finally contacted.

We can't afford to let 25 percent of our customers live in the Dark Ages. "Do something, quick!" cried our client. Well, not so fast. Consider a couple of quick caveats before we proceed:

1. **No Surprises.**

    We should make sure that customers are not surprised to get a text message. In their Loyalty Program Membership Application, the retailer had specific language informing the customer that they would be contacted via cell phone or text messaging if they gave their cell phone number as a contact. Industry best practices require a customer to have opted in to receive text messages.

2. **Don't Overstay the Welcome.**

    We must provide a way for the customer to tell us that they don't want to receive text messaging in the future. Best practices require that any customer receiving a text message can easily opt out from receiving future contacts.

As we might expect, the second point makes many marketers' knees tremble. "But my customers will opt out and leave me with no way of communicating with them …"

It's true. Some will leave, and we should be thankful they did. That's one less unresponsive customer on which to expend money and effort. We don't want to corral customers, as if once they're in, there's no way out.

Besides, the "opt out" numbers are rarely significant. For this test campaign, we're talking about two out of every 1,000 customers contacted. That's 2/10 of one percent. Opt outs for voice messaging are about half of that number. This is not something to lose sleep over.

On the bright side, a whopping 97 percent of all text messages delivered are opened and read, and 80 percent of them are read within an hour of delivery. Can you imagine the kind of responses we would generate for direct mail with stats like that?

Even better, text messaging provides some unique opportunities for customer communication. For example, we could ask the customer to save the text message in his/her cell phone. Then he or she could come to the store, and simply show the message on their phone to the cashier for a discount. Kiss those coupons, goodbye.

Line	Sample Text Message
1	Hurry to
2	
3	XYZ Company
4	
5	20% off 1 item
6	
7	25% off 2 items
8	
9	33% off 3 items
10	
11	FRIDAY ONLY!
12	
13	Show this message
14	
15	2 get discount
16	
17	Reply w/STOP to
18	
19	opt out

Cute, huh? The size is about what will fit on a phone's screen, and the number of characters is 160 characters or less.

It looks great. It sounds great. But does it work? You tell me.

We sent over 500,000 of these text messages for a cost of about $50,000. Those who responded generated measurable sales of more than $600,000. Would our CFO spend $50,000 to generate $600,000 in sales? He would do it any day of the week and twice on Sunday. At keystone margin, it was a 500 percent ROI in a matter of a few days.

My Suggestion:

Act now b4 it's 2 late. There r $$$ in nu mail.

Technology marches on.

Chapter IX

September—Harvest Time

(Wk 1: Seeding files)

It's true. You can take the boy off the farm, but you'll never get the farm out of the boy. For someone like me, born and raised in Boone, North Carolina, I can't help but think of September as that time of year when the "chickens come home to roost" and you reap what you've sown. It's harvest time, once again.

That's not a bad time for us to roll-up our sleeves, look at our own CRM crop, and apply a little down-home wisdom to our communication efforts. We finished the summer with a look at the latest in new technologies. In September, let's go back to some old-fashioned ideas—and talk about seeding, pruning, and checking to see what made it into the barn. So ...

To seed or not to seed, that is the question.

Now, how many farm boys can quote (or at least misquote) Shakespeare? While you're pondering the meaning of seeding, let me reassure you: there's no need for a quick trip to the local feed store, or the biology lab either. Good seed for the retailer is all about a "seed file". Trust me on this; we all have a need for seed.

A seed file is a group of *interested parties*, normally employees, who receive the direct mail communication during a marketing campaign. Seed files are used primarily in direct mail, but should be considered for voice messaging and email messaging, as well.

"Hmm. Let's get this straight. These are people over and above the customers who meet the selection criteria—people who are not customers or potential customers—to whom we are now going to send our precious and expensive postcards. Fill us in, Claude. Why are we doing this?"

So glad you asked. Now let me ask a question:

How do we know that the mailing got to the customers on time and in the proper condition?

Here's a war story, straight from the front lines:

A few years ago, a client contracted with a mailing house to print and mail about 400,000 pieces. The mail house was well-respected in the industry and had been reliable in the past. However, this mail piece was more complicated, with a larger quantity, and a very specific date by which it had to be in the customers' hands.

As that date came and went, the stores reported no sales for the customers on the mailing list. Not a good start. Days passed. Nothing. Frantic, the marketing department telephoned the stores. Surely, they must be doing something wrong!

But here's a surprise ending: it turns out that the stores weren't doing anything wrong (or at least nothing to do with the mail campaign). After all else failed, someone thought to contact the mail house. This is what they learned:

1) The piece was so complicated for the mail house that the "first batch" had only just been mailed, several days after the deadline by which the customer needed to receive the piece.

2) The balance of the pieces would be going out piecemeal over the next several weeks.

This little mistake cost the retailer over a million dollars in sales.

The moral of the story is: don't assume that the mail house always gets it right. Trust, but verify. That's what a seed file does.

We start by creating a list of employees/executives and anointing them Seed File Members. Don't worry, there's no need for special initiation rites, sprinkling of oils, or secret vows of seed loyalty. In fact our seed file should be completely indistinguishable (big word for a country boy) from regular customers when it's submitted to the mail house. The best solution of all is to mix up the seed file with the customer file receiving the mail piece.

Why all the cloak and dagger? Think about it. If we identify the Seed List separately when we submit it to the mail house, we may as well have stamped it "IMPORTANT: Handle These People With SPECIAL Care". If a problem exists at the mail house, they will give priority to the Seed List to hide any problems from the retailer. The whole purpose of the seed list is to measure the effectiveness of the mail house for our regular customers. We don't need to provide a VIP list.

This is not to say that our Seed File members themselves should be undistinguished. Depending on the retailer and the involvement of executives in the program, the file should include the President, and continue down the chain of command. Certainly, some marketing personnel should be included, so that they can see the condition of the piece and the date of arrival.

At the very least, the Seed File should be made up of a few store operations personnel spread across the geography where the stores are located. Many of my clients include every store manager in the file, as it allows the managers to see the mail piece at the same time as their customers. Everyone in the Seed File is required to email back the date of arrival, and any comments about the condition of the piece.

Obviously, a Seed File will not stop mistakes. But it will alert the organization to production issues or delivery delays, while there is still time to react. If a problem occurs for the Seed File members, it is surely happening for our customers as well. We'd better jump on it quickly.

To seed or not to seed?

My Suggestion:
　　SEED, SEED, SEED.

Establish a seed file immediately, and react to problems as soon as you find them. The only bad seed is no seed at all!

(Wk 2: Pruning & measuring)

Have you ever been to a Harvest festival—those charming rural events where farmers compete to grow the biggest squash or the plumpest pumpkin? Seems like fun to city folks. But to the locals, it can be a pretty heated competition. After all, no matter where they are or what business they're in, people want to know how they stack up.

It's even true when it comes to assessing our CRM results. We need a yardstick to measure ourselves against. After all, if you'd never seen a normal size squash, how would you recognize a particularly big one? No farmer takes credit for an orange pumpkin. That's just how nature grows them. Did we sell more last weekend because of something we did, or the luck of the draw? We have to compare ourselves to something in order to know how we're faring, and to determine if it's our efforts, or the laws of nature, that are getting us there.

Here's another war story—this one straight from the corporate boardroom, at the Monday morning meeting.

A client in the Midwest regularly sent 24-page mini-catalogs to its customers. In this specific case, the retailer selected 257,724 customers who had purchased in the last 12 months and who lived in the states in which the company had stores. Naturally, the customers were tracked during the event. 24,832 of the customers who received the mailing purchased, for a total of $4,769,234 and an average transaction of $192.06.

Measured Results

257,724	Quantity Mailed
24,832	# of Responses
9.6%	Response Rate
$192.06	Average Transaction Dollars
$4,769,234	Total Sales

What can I say? When you're good, you're good.

Sometimes though, you don't get quite the pat on the back that you were expecting. In the face of such glowing results, there has to be a naysayer. This role is usually filled by our friend, the CFO.

At a Monday morning meeting the following month, this CFO couldn't help noting that sales had been very soft for a week or two *after* the event. He had his own explanation. The sales that had been generated by the mailing were a mirage. "Those were our best customers and they would have come in without that mini-catalog," he decided. As far as he could tell, the marketing department had simply moved the sales forward by a couple of weeks.

As this was back before I knew better, I attempted to prove the validity of the results by highlighting comparisons of this year versus last year, or this month versus last month, or sales trends, or anything else I could muster. The CFO would hear none of it. "They would have come in any way," he declared. I couldn't help wondering how newspaper, radio, and TV advertising had been able to slip past this hurdle for so many years. But wisely, I kept my thoughts to myself. It's good to have a little control.

No, not self-control. That's good too. But in this case, what we needed was a control file—a measuring stick that would allow us to validate our results, even to an audience of skeptics. Of course, we know which customers have been targeted with a mail piece and which ones did not receive it. The trick then is to randomly select a number of customers who would normally receive the mail piece and intentionally *not* send it to them. Now we can track their purchase patterns. Any difference between the mailed group and the non-mailed group (the control file) will show the effect of the mail piece.

In this particular instance, we were fortunate that the retailer's marketing executive knew about control groups. Prior to the mailing, he had selected all the customers who had purchased in the last 12 months, then randomly selected 25,781 customers not to mail. The balance (257,724 customers) received the mailing. Below, you can see that many of the retailer's customers actually did come into the stores without having received the mini-catalog.

Control File Measurement

25,781	Control Quantity
1,703	# of Purchasers
6.6%	Response Rate
$163.06	Average Transaction Dollars
$277,691	Total Sales

But the crucial statistics here are the Incremental Response Rate and Average Response Dollars. The mailed group had an increase of 3.0% and an average spend of $29.00, respectively.

Incremental over Control

3.0%	Response Rate
$29.00	Average Response Dollars

The impact of the extra 3.0 percent response rate and extra average transaction of $29.00 was a total incremental sales increase of $2,205,082.

Incremental over Control

$2,205,082	Total Sales

That ain't chicken feed, my friend. This mini-catalog cost about $125,000 to produce and mail. It generated $2.2 million in incremental sales. Let's go back to next week's meeting and ask our CFO if he might want to reconsider, and do that event again next year.

My Suggestion:

When people question your results, don't get mad.

Don't get even. Get control. Always set up a control group for any CRM initiative—this is how we measure our results.

(Wk 3: Weighing the results)

Let's go back to that Harvest Festival one more time. Have another piece of pie. Try some local brew. Buy a souvenir or two. We've still got something more to learn.

If you grew up near a farm like I did, you know that farmers don't throw much away. Nothing in the harvest process has just one use. Got pumpkins? Make a pie. But save the seeds—you can use those too. Growing corn? Sure, you want the ear. But hold onto those husks as well. Tourists love those cute little dolls that Grandma makes out of the dried corn husks.

Looking at the results of that catalog mailing from last week, the one where we generated more than 2 million dollars in sales over the "control" file, a lot of retailers would grab their money and run. But when we're counting up our results, there's more to it than just gathering the greenbacks and clearing the field. We need to separate the proverbial wheat from the chaff, and glean all we can from what we've grown. There's more out there to be harvested, and what's left is just as valuable as money. It's information!

In last week's example, the mail file averaged 3 percent over the control file. The control file is the selected group of customers who were not mailed the catalog. Even the ever-skeptical CFO had to concede that the event was a success. But quite rightly, he wanted to know more. Where did the success come from? What could be done with it? Certainly, within that 3 percent average, there were segments of customers who averaged more or less. Knowing which customer segments are at the different extremes is where the real learning begins.

So how do we make use of all, not just a part, of the information that we've gathered from our CRM event? The key is to divide and conquer. We're best to do it before, not after, the event.

Once the mail file has been pulled and sent to the mail house, we can break it into smaller pieces, or segments, based on a criterion that will fit our needs. In the case of the Midwest retailer from last week, we broke out segments according to monetary value—that is, the dollar amount of the customer's purchases over the last 12 months.

Luckily, this retailer had their fundamental CRM structure in place. We have to be able to identify segments, create them from the mailing list, place each customer in the correct segment, and measure each customer's response. If we can't do that, then much of our opportunity for information gathering is lost.

Seg	12-Month Purchase Segments	Mailed
1	$1-249	13,519
2	$250-499	71,366
3	$500-999	66,715
4	$1,000-1,499	32,450
5	$1,500-2,499	32,035
6	$2,500-3,499	15,054
7	$3,500-4,999	11,163
8	$5,000+	15,422
	Total----->	257,724

Now, I know this CRM stuff is exciting, but this is no time to lose control. Even within each monetary category, we need a yardstick for judging our results. As we can see below, the retailer pulled a control file for each segment, and tracked the results of the control file against the mail file:

Seg	12-Month Purchase Segments	Mailed	Response Rate Mail	Control	Avg. Trans. Mail	Control
1	$1-249	13,519	2.60%	2.10%	$126.22	$177.79
2	$250-499	71,366	3.70%	3.00%	$139.84	$121.05
3	$500-999	66,715	6.40%	4.40%	$148.31	$144.28
4	$1,000-1,499	32,450	9.70%	6.20%	$166.75	$171.45
5	$1,500-2,499	32,035	13.60%	8.30%	$170.74	$146.19
6	$2,500-3,499	15,054	17.80%	10.80%	$194.42	$179.08
7	$3,500-4,999	11,163	22.30%	14.70%	$209.61	$160.28
8	$5,000+	15,422	31.80%	23.70%	$288.15	$204.91
	Total------->	257,724	9.60%	6.60%	$192.05	$163.97

The good news is: each monetary segment outperformed the control file in response rate. The not so good news is: for Segment 1 ($1–249), the average transaction of the control file actually exceeded that of the mailed file. Here are the rest of the findings:

Seg	12-Month Purchase Segments	Mailed	Total Sales		Event Profit
			Mailed	Incremental	
1	$1-249	13,519	$44,177	$ (6,297)	$ (9,278)
2	$250-499	71,366	$367,791	$ 110,971	$ 8,705
3	$500-999	66,715	$635,342	$ 209,599	$ 50,482
4	$1,000-1,499	32,450	$527,253	$ 182,127	$ 56,626
5	$1,500-2,499	32,035	$742,039	$ 354,873	$ 125,932
6	$2,500-3,499	15,054	$520,646	$ 229,242	$ 84,170
7	$3,500-4,999	11,163	$521,090	$ 258,077	$ 97,649
8	$5,000+	15,422	$1,410,782	$ 661,833	$ 257,022
	Total-------->	257,724	$4,769,121	$2,000,425	$671,308

Not everything comes up roses. In fact, Segment 1 ($1–249) actually lost sales. In the last column, we can see that this segment had a negative event profit. In case that term is new to anyone, event profit is calculated as: incremental gross margin dollars minus the cost of the event. In this case, that meant a negative incremental sales number multiplied by a 40 percent margin, minus the cost of the mail piece.

$$($6,297) \quad \times \quad 40\% \quad - \quad $6760 \quad = \quad ($9,278)$$

(inc. sales)   (margin)   (mail piece cost)   (event profit)

Not too surprisingly, the CFO thought that this response from Segment 1 was not such a good thing. He suggested that something be done about it in the future.

But we can also see that Segment 8 ($5,000+) created about as much profit as all the other segments combined. The CFO said this was a very good thing. He thought maybe we should be talking more to these folks in the future. Or even better, we could try to find some more customers just like them.

The CFO might be on to something there. When we look at only the top line results of an event, we lose sight of the details. The profit is in the details.

There is a barometer used in CRM called: Sales to Cost Ratio (incremental sales divided by the cost of the event). The Sales to Cost Ratio for this mini-catalog event was quite impressive: $15.52. But if Segment 1 had not been mailed, the ratio would have been a whopping $16.43. The CFO would definitely approve.

Don't stop analyzing too soon. Once we've made one segment, we can break that down further into even more precise segments. For example, we wouldn't want to simply eliminate Segment 1, just because of the 2.1% average response rate. After all, the average for this segment is no different than the overall average. There will be smaller segments within this segment that exceeded 2.1 percent (and might have even exceeded the breakeven point for the event). Never throw anything away. The farmer who can glean the smaller segments, and harvest them effectively is the one with a barn full of profits.

Back at the Monday morning meeting, the CFO had one last question. "If we are making all this money mailing the customers, why are we not mailing to the control file as well?"

"Uh, because we had to be able to prove that the event generated incremental sales and profits", Claude stammered …

The CFO persevered, "Well, how large does this control file need to be? These are our customers. If we can make money mailing them, let's mail as many as we can …"

My Suggestion:

Do some pruning.

Identify the segments that responded well and keep communicating to them. Identify the segments that responded poorly and eliminate them.

(Wk 4: Size DOES matter)

When we last tuned in, Claude and his merry band of CRM practitioners had just escaped a challenge from the CFO to their very impressive event results (over 2 million dollars in sales and a $192 average purchase) through careful use of the control file. Confronted with a comparison between the results of the mailed file and the control file, which showed a marked 3 percent difference in incremental sales generated, the CFO was forced to admit that the event had been a success.

But no one gets off that easy. Before he lets everyone out of the Monday morning meeting, the CFO has one more question he wants answered:

"Does size matter?"

Hmm. This one had better be handled with care. What exactly are we talking about?

Certainly, size matters. If we're talking about harvesting our results, big yields are better than small ones. If we're counting our profits, the more the merrier. If we're calculating year-end bonuses, a whole lot is better than a little. Not much argument there. Does size matter? Is this a trick question?

Maybe. Size does indeed matter. That doesn't mean that bigger is always better. When we're talking control files, we don't want the Size Extra, Extra Large. We also don't want a Size Petite. We need a size that fits, and overshooting the mark will not leave us with better information. It will deprive us of bigger profits.

This is what the CFO was on to (these guys catch on pretty fast). Once he saw the sizeable difference in incremental sales between the mailed file and the controlled file, he immediately wanted to know if the control file had to be as big as it was. After all, if more of those Control File customers had been mailed, and if they had the same response rate and average transaction as the Mailed File, it would have generated significantly more sales. How much more? Stay tuned. Don't touch that dial.

In our next scene, we follow Claude back into his CRM laboratory, where he mixes his secret potions, creates his mad inventions, and of course puts the lab rats through their paces. Let's join Claude as he searches desperately for the answer to that mystery that has so long perplexed the world:

How Big Should The Control File Be?

Well, I suppose that's not exactly how the scene played out. But I did do some research on this. I read books and magazine articles. I looked through my college statistics texts. I interviewed several people with PhD's in marketing and statistics. After all that, I discovered:

No one knows. Or, no one knows exactly. That bit about the mystery that has perplexed the world is pretty much true. There is no universal method for determining the size of the control file. In fact, most people who are "database marketing professionals" don't have a clue how to calculate this.

I was in uncharted territory here, but I was well aware of the dangers. First of all, I knew that whatever number was selected, there would be those who would second-guess it as being too large—particularly CFO's who like to calculate the amount of sales lost in the control file. I also knew there would be even more people who would deem the magic number too small. If the results of a mail event are not great, the stakeholders in the event will almost always second-guess the control file results, rather than the problems with the event itself.

But even in the face of peril, I persisted, venturing where no retail CRM expert had gone before. In the end, it came down to a simple formula:

Control Group Calculation

Control group size is based on an expected response rate and the desired statistical viability of the results. The following calculation can be used to determine a statistically valid control group size

$$m = t^2pq/d^2$$

Where m = Control File Size

t = Confidence Level

(number of times out of 100 attempts the prediction must be correct)

Most common "t" values

1.282—90% confidence level

1.645—95% confidence level

2.326—99% confidence level

p = probability of response

q – probability of non-response

d = significance of the result

    (typically .5% half a percent)

Don't panic. This is simpler than it looks. Let's get it out of the abstract, and put this into the real world. To use the formula above:

a)   determine the amount of confidence you wish to have in the result, and

b)   estimate the response rate for the direct marketing event.

Every marketer I know will accept a 90 percent confidence level. With the exception of death and taxes, not much else in life rates beyond a 90 percent sure bet, so this number seems reasonable. In this particular case then, t=1.282

Similarly, if we've executed similar direct mail events in the past, we can estimate the response rate with a reasonably high degree of accuracy. Quite frankly, if we miss it by a few percentage points, it will not sink the ship. In this particular case, the Director of Database Marketing had done several catalogs over the past few years, and estimated a 6 percent response rate. (The actual response turned out to be 9.6 percent).

With those values plugged into the formula, you will see that the control file size is calculated at 3,708 customer records.

90% confidence level

$m = (1.282)^2(.06)(.94)/(.005)^2$

$m = 3{,}708$ control file records

If we wanted to increase our confidence level from 90 percent to 95 percent, it's a simple matter of plugging the new numbers into the formula.

95% confidence level

$m = (1.645)^2(.06)(.94)/(.005)^2$

$m = 6{,}105$ control file records

There are those who may want 95 percent confidence, but it's worth asking "at what cost?" Personally, I prefer the Control File be as small as possible and still statistically accurate. I want as many customers as possible to get the mail piece and respond at the higher rate and average transaction. Why else are we doing all this work?

Don't ask me to defend this formula or try to explain all the science behind it. Statisticians have presented doctoral theses on this subject. I'm just a poor boy from the mountains of North Carolina. But I did have some "schooling'" in statistics at an undergraduate and graduate level—enough to recognize when a formula works.

Size matters all right, just ask our CFO …

"Hey, wait a minute" the CFO roars. "Did you just tell us that our Control File for that event should have been 3,708 customers? How big was our control file anyway?" A familiar, foreboding silence engulfs the crowded meeting room.

A small voice pipes up from the back of the room. "Our Control File was 25, 781 customers, sir". A collective gasp is heard.

"Oh my.… Twenty-five thousand? What the …?" the CFO blusters, his face turning as red as the ink on a balance sheet. "That's 21,000 customers we could have mailed to! And what did this little blunder cost us, I wonder?"

My Suggestion:
    Try it.

Guessing about the size of your control file is much too expensive. Use the formula, and a healthy helping of common sense, to control the size of your control file, and figure out how big is big enough.

Like I said … don't touch that dial.

(Wk 5: Bigger doesn't always mean better)

All month long, we've been discussing the challenges of harvesting our results. Seeding, gathering, measuring, pruning and counting is all a part of the harvest season, and as any farm boy knows, this is when the score gets tallied. Whatever transpired the rest of the year; this is when the scales hang in the balance. For better or worse, we find ourselves reaping what we've sown.

Remember last week's vexing question from the CFO? As good as the numbers for that direct mail event appeared, generating 2 million dollars in sales and a $192 average transaction, there was a fly in the ointment. After estimating that the control file size for the mailing should have been 3,708 customers, the CFO was informed that the actual size of the control file was 25,781 customers. This meant there were 22,073 customers who could have received the mail piece, but did not.

Put on your overalls, people. Something is about to hit the fan.

The CFO asked, "How much did this miscalculation in the control file cost us?"

Actual Control Size	25,781
Calculated Control Size	3,708
Quantity Available to Mail	22,073

We can start with the assumption that these 22,073 control file customers would have responded at the same rate as the mailed file, which is to say at an incremental increase of 3 percent. After all, the control file was selected from the larger, mailed file. Statistically, there is no reason that these customers would not have responded in the same manner as the rest of the people in the mailed file. Quite simply, we lost 3.0% of the incremental response rate or 662 transactions.

Financial Impact

Incremental Response Rate	3.0%
Incremental Transactions if Mailed	662

Further, these customers would have averaged the same expenditures as the mailed file, which had an average transaction of $192.06. That little miscalculation in the size of the control file caused a loss of $127,180. It appears that bigger is not always better. We've paid a heavy price for having a control file that was larger than statistically required.

Financial Impact

Incremental Response Rate	3.0%
Incremental Transactions if Mailed	662
Average Transaction Dollars	$192.06
Lost Sales	$127,180

Let's take it a little further. This retailer normally mails 5 similar catalogs per year. If this mistake had not been caught, the annual lost sales could have topped $600,000, just for those 5 catalogs. Throw in a few postcards and letters and we have close to a million dollars a year. That clucking sound you hear around the boardroom table might be the proverbial chickens finally coming home to roost.

Of course, next time we'll use our formula for determining the size of the control file. No more guesswork in matters like this. We'll rely on the cold hard scientific formula, right?

Well, gather round and let me share one more bit of down-home wisdom before we put this month to bed.

We can also use a little common sense.

Remember that stuff? It comes in very handy when the numbers in the formula don't quite add up. Here's an example:

Having determined the required level of confidence and the expected response, we calculate the size of the control file to be 3,708 customers. Then, using very specific selection criteria, we select a total of 4,000 customers who qualify for the mailing. Do we really subtract 3,708 customers out of this group, as a control file? We would only be mailing to 292 customers. What to do? Use some common sense. Make a business decision to go without a control file.

In my research on the use of control files, I spoke to a very interesting professor of marketing at Northwestern University. He went through all the calculations, "use this variable, use this constant, use this level of confidence" and on and on. After all that, he said, "And use a large portion of common sense."

Here are a couple pearls of wisdom to keep in mind:

1) Nothing happens overnight. And time is money. Control files take time to pull, manage, measure and report on.

2) You can't mix apples and oranges. The size of the control file has no relationship to the size of the mail file. In fact, the mail file and its size are not even addressed in the formula for control size calculation.

3) Bigger is not always better. But neither is smaller. If we're pulling control files using 10 percent of the mail file, when the mail file is less than 37,080, all we're really making is work. At that point, the numbers are too small to accurately impact our decision-making. Are we really going to make any far-reaching determinations on a control file of 100 customers? Or 200? Or 500?

4) Use it or lose it. If our organization is not going to make any decisions as a result of comparing the mail file to the control file, then let's not bother with it. I know a respected speaker in CRM who says, "You must have a control file for every mailing." Hogwash. Use some measure of common sense.

5) Don't change horses in mid-stream. The comparison of the mailed file to the control file is the comparison of the total mailing results to the total control results. If we want to compare a subset of the total mail file to the total control file, the rules do not apply. During the next mailing, we can pull a control file out of the subset for comparison. Still, we have to keep in mind that the size of that control file must be calculated using the same formula.

When it comes to gathering results, the greatest harvest is information—accurate, useful, relevant information. A seed file will show us when our mailing is arriving to customers, and how it looks when it gets there. A control file will give us a measuring stick to calculate our results. Used wisely, the control file will tell us how well we did. But used too widely, the control file will also carry a cost.

My Suggestion:

   Use seed files and control files to monitor the success of CRM initiatives.

Then, use a little calculation and a little common sense as well. Keep the control files as small as possible to maximize results.

Chapter X

October—The dark and stormy night

(Wk 1: Twins of terror)

It was a dark and stormy night....

Everyone likes a scary story, especially at this time of year. We don't want anything too frightening for the kids—just a friendly ghost here and there, an old lady in a pointy hat riding around on a broom. Everyone likes the occasional tale from the dark side.

So step right up folks, and check out Crazy Claude's House of Horrors. Enter if you dare, and witness the terrors of CRM gone awry. Communication breakdowns of all sizes and shapes; ghosts in the machines, tangled webs of government bureaucracy, empty houses with buyers still haunted by events gone horribly wrong ...

Welcome to my nightmare! This month, we're not looking on the bright side. Instead, let's face our demons—all those things that endanger the communication between us and our customers. Granted, it's not always a pretty picture. Still, better the devil we know, than the unexpected bump in the night. So dim the lights, and witness our first feature:

DOUBLEdoubleVISIONvision *"Beware the Evil Twin"*

How scary are duplicates in our data? Not very scary, right? In the end, they increase the number of customer records on the database. That's a good thing, isn't it?

Don't be too sure. It always starts out so innocently ...

One fine June day, Claude Johnson stops by our quiet little store, to make a purchase. Being the model CRM citizens that we are, we immediately create a customer record for our new friend Claude, which includes his name and address. Then, we attach Claude's purchase history to that record.

What happens when Claude comes back during July and buys some more stuff?

That's easy. We use our software at POS (or on the web/call center) to match Claude's July purchases to the customer record we made back in June. By doing this, we can easily recognize that Claude is becoming a very good customer. We can even reward him for his loyalty. Unless …

Unless something goes wrong. Even with our best-laid plans, someone in the store or the web/call center has to take the time to find Claude's June record, and attach the July sale. What if one of our employees is insufficiently motivated, inadequately trained, or just too busy to follow procedures that would match Claude's June and July transactions?

Uh oh. Something bad is about to happen. Can you hear the low, ominous rumbling of the cellos and the trombones?

The result of our failure to match transactions is:

(a) The July sale has no customer information at all, and gets thrown in the "no customer information bucket" along with lots of other transactions. All contact lost.

(b) The store associate creates a new record for Claude, reflecting the July transaction. OH NO! IT'S HERE:

The dreaded **Duplicate Customer Record**. Meet Claude Johnson's Evil Twin.

A lot of us have them. For one particular client, I extracted all the customer records created during the past four months that were part of a duplicate set. In fact, some were not merely duplicates, but triplicates. It's ugly work, but someone has to do it. The chart below reflects the 2,822 customers: customers with the same last name and address. It was about 4 percent of the database.

| Customers with duplicate records on file | | | | | |
| Exact duplicate address and last name | | | | | |
Monetary Segment	Cust Count	% of Total	Lifetime Purchases	% of Total	Avg Spend
Diamond	331	11.7%	$ 2,016,978	57.2%	$ 6,094
Ruby	399	14.1%	$ 556,203	15.8%	$ 1,394
Opal	945	33.5%	$ 549,738	15.6%	$ 582
Pearl	1,147	40.6%	$ 402,885	11.4%	$ 351
Total	2,822		$ 3,525,804		$ 1,249

We should notice that the distribution of customers according to the client's definition of Diamond, Ruby, Opal, and Pearl monetary segments is relatively normal. We can also note that the average lifetime spend per customer is $1,249.

These are all duplicate sets. So what would happen if we were to merge the duplicate records' purchase history and eliminate the duplicate customer records? For the purposes of this case study, I merged the older customer record into the newer one. The result is most interesting.

- The customer count went down by 1,439 records. This is neither good news nor bad news. This is reality. It's better we see things as they really are.

- The dollars stayed the same. This is a good thing. Duplication doesn't make us any money. It only costs us money.

- The Average Lifetime Spend per customer went up by $2,549. This is a very good thing. Our customer is more loyal, and spends more than we ever knew!

Admittedly, this example is based on a small number of records. However, I have clients who, when we got them to look at duplicates, found over a hundred thousand duplicates. The truth is that only a very small percentage of retail customers ever end up having 2 or more transactions. The DMA says that less than 50% first time buyers come back for a second transaction. All of these 1,383 customers are in that repeat customer category, else they would not have a duplicate record. They are the most important targets in our CRM efforts.

In the next chart, we can see the distribution of the 2,822 customers according to their monetary/recency segment before the merger of accounts. Below that, we see the resultant 1,383 customers in the same grid, now that the records have been merged. Be sure to notice how the accounts moved from segment to segment.

Customers with duplicate records on file					
Exact duplicate address and last name					
Monetary Segment	Cust Count	% of Total	Lifetime Purchases	% of Total	Avg Spend
Diamond	331	11.7%	$ 2,016,978	57.2%	$ 6,094
Ruby	399	14.1%	$ 556,203	15.8%	$ 1,394
Opal	945	33.5%	$ 549,738	15.6%	$ 582
Pearl	1,147	40.6%	$ 402,885	11.4%	$ 351
Total	**2,822**		**$ 3,525,804**		**$ 1,249**

After merger of duplicate records					
Monetary Segment	Cust Count	% of Total	Lifetime Purchases	% of Total	Avg Spend
Diamond	398	28.8%	$ 2,733,700	77.5%	$ 6,869
Ruby	329	23.8%	$ 474,685	13.5%	$ 1,443
Opal	457	33.0%	$ 283,696	8.0%	$ 621
Pearl	199	14.4%	$ 33,724	1.0%	$ 169
Total	**1,383**		**$ 3,525,804**		**$ 2,549**

Before the records were merged, 64 percent of the accounts made their last purchase in the past 6 months. After the merger, that percentage went up to 92 percent. That's not too surprising, since the duplicate records were created in the last 4 months.

This is the cost of Double Vision: our perception is blurred. Before the above merger took place, the retailer's CRM Manager thought 1,439 customers were all new customers. There weren't. Instead, there were 1,439 *returning* customers—people who had made previous purchases, and whose most recent purchase was in the last 3 to 6 months. Moreover, these customers were more important than they appeared to be. Their lifetime purchase amount was double what the original records indicated.

All of our CRM work is based on information. We're only as good as the information that we have. Different information generates different marketing decisions. Different subsets of customers require different communication. If we have a database full of "evil twins", we can't expect to communicate accurately and effectively. We won't know who we're talking to.

"Ah, Claude. You don't scare us. That sort of thing could never happen here ..."

Sure. A couple of years ago, I worked with a client who had over 1.4 million records on their customer database. When asked about any efforts to identify or merge duplicates, the client replied confidently, "our database marketing software is supposed to take care of that". Right. And Freddie Kruger was supposed to be dead after the first movie.

We sent that client's database to a third party processor, who uncovers duplicates using very sophisticated identification logic. They turned up 114,000 "evil twins" lurking out there—almost 10 percent of the database.

How safe do you feel now?

My Suggestion:

> **Don't leave these evil customer records alone in the dark.**

They'll only multiply. Soon they'll be snatching energy, money and results from your CRM efforts. Root them out. Expose them. Merge them with their better half. Don't let double vision do you in ...

(Wk 2: Phone terror [Do Not Call registry])

<u>**Act 1 Scene 1 "They Only Ring Once"**</u>

Location: Kitchen Time: Night

A YOUNG WOMAN in an apron works in silence, chopping vegetables …

A POT of sauce simmers on the stove.

Just as she's bringing the knife down on those vegetables …

A TELEPHONE RINGS!

THE WOMAN jumps, startled by the sound …

"Ow!!" She cuts herself. Cursing under her breath, she runs to the phone …

WOMAN

(Picking up)

Honey … please don't tell me you're going to be late. You won't believe the meal I'm cooking up here …

(She nurses her hand, trying to stop the bleeding)

Hello? Harold? Are you there? Harold?

A VOICE (OFF STAGE)

(on the phone)

Good evening. This is Brad from XYZ Windows and Siding.

THE POT—it's reached a boiling point. Bubbling up over the edge and onto the stove …

A VOICE (O.S.) (Continued)

Are you aware that at this moment, Hurricane Hattie is headed up the coast toward your home? Now may be your last chance to purchase the storm windows that can protect your investment …

WOMAN

(exasperated)

What? We rent in an apartment building. Why are you bothering?

(as she turns around …)

Oh no! My sauce …

THERE OUGHTTA BE A LAW! Well, @#!%#! There is!

The National Do Not Call registry was created to offer consumers a choice as to whether or not they wish to receive telemarketing calls. It was the culmination of a 3-year review by the Federal Trade Commission of the Telemarketing Sales Rule. Simply stated, the Do Not Call provisions of the Telemarketing Sales Rule cover any plan, program or campaign to sell goods or services through interstate phone calls.

Here's the scary part:

That means *you*, dear retailer. Our CRM strategy just got a little more compli-cated. If we fail to comply with a consumer's request to remove their name from our call list, or if we call a consumer despite the fact that he or she is on the Do Not Call registry, we could face an $11,000 fine.

As is to be expected in a law drawn up by politicians, some groups have been granted exemptions from the rules—political organizations are among those who are exempt. So rest easy, we can still receive those pre-election telephone greetings from the mayor, or the President of the United States telling us whom we should vote for (does anyone make up his or her mind the night before the election?). Charities, telephone surveyors, and companies with whom the consumer has an existing business relationship are also exempt.

So where does this leave us in communicating with our customers, or potential customers?

It leaves us with a pretty strict set of guidelines:

- We CAN phone those people who are not on the Do Not Call registry.
- We CAN phone those people on the Do Not Call registry with whom we have some established relationship.

- We CANNOT phone those on the registry with whom we do not have a relationship.

- We CANNOT phone those on the registry with whom we had a past relationship if the customer's last purchase, delivery or payment was over 18 months ago. The FTC has finally settled the debate among retailers of what constitutes customer retention, setting the official line at 18 months.

What about new customers? How do we go after them?

Quickly, that's how. There is a window of opportunity during which we are allowed to contact a potential customer, even if their numbers are on the Do Not Call Registry—if they have inquired about one of our products or services. However, that window doesn't stay open for long. We have 3 months to approach, nurture and hopefully create a relationship. It's like speed dating for retailers.

Confused yet? That was the simple, straightforward part. Now, we have to figure out into which category each of our customers should be placed. How can we know who's on the Do Not Call Registry?

Here's some bedtime reading for you: a piece of government literature, containing over fifty million telephone numbers that WE CAN'T CALL. It's like being given cake, with instructions never to eat it. These customers are off-limits. To paraphrase Johnnie Cochran: **If they are a Do Not Call requester, we must not pester.** It's up to us to obtain this information, and keep it updated. Every 3 months, we need to synchronize our Do Not Call list with a new version of the registry, which we can access at www.telemarketing.donotcall.gov.

When we visit the site, we'll be asked to provide identifying information about our comp-any, in order to obtain an account number. This entitles us to visit as often as we please for one year. We'll start by downloading the file (which consists of sorted telephone numbers) for the zip codes we select. On subsequent visits, we can simply download changes in the data that have occurred since our last visit. Luckily, the website does a pretty good job of keeping that straight for us.

"Of course, this is all free, right? Certainly, the government isn't planning on charging us for the privilege of purchasing a long list of phone numbers that we can't call....

I warned you that this was a scary story. Free downloads are only available for the first 5 area codes (not exactly a sweeping CRM campaign). Beyond the initial 5, there is an annual fee of $25 per area code of data, along with an annual fee of

$7,375 for the entire US database. One has to wonder how they come up with this stuff. I picture a highly paid government statistical analyst conferring with a macro-economist, as they sit in a dark corner with an abacus, searching for the magic number that will fund the federal deficit on the backs of the telemarketers.

If we really want something that will keep us up at night, let's imagine the potential for inadvertent mistakes. With a price tag of $11,000 per customer, and the possibility of civil penalties or sanctions, errors could get pretty pricey. The best protection is preparation. We'd better be sure that we have procedures in place to comply with the ruling.

My Suggestion:

> **Take the basic steps that show a good faith effort to comply with do Not Call Legislation.**

That means:

- Written procedures for the staff to comply
- Evidence of training for personnel
- Efforts to monitor and enforce compliance
- Maintenance of a "company specific" Do Not Call list
- Records of when we have accessed the National Registry web site
- Willingness to call in our own violations when we err.

(Wk 3: Technology terror [SPAM])

Did you ever start to feel like one of those hapless heroines trapped in the crucial moments of a slasher movie?

You reach out to your friend to come to the rescue …
But it's your friend's Evil Twin!
You race to the phone to call for help.…
But the lines have been cut!
You jump on the computer, trying to email a desperate SOS to someone … anyone …
But your email is blocked!

Help!! All communication has broken down! We're entirely cut off from the outside world!!

Well, maybe not entirely. But when it comes to a retailer's ability to communicate with customers, these are the best of times, and the worst of times. They are the best of times because we have more venues for communication than ever before—not just direct mail, and phone calls, but emailing, voice-mail messaging, text messaging, and on and on.

They are the worst of times because we have to deal with 2 different challenges at once. We must fight against those who would abuse the access provided by these new forms of communication. At the same time, we must struggle to adapt to the restrictions placed on us by the federal government, as we market to our customers.

First, there was the Do Not Call Registry. Now they're after SPAM.

Not the Hormel Spam on the grocery shelf. No one is after that. The Feds are out to stop the spam that's popping up and clogging up our email inbox, and in some instances, fogging up our judgment with "get rich quick" schemes or fraudulent business offers.

In an effort to clear our mailboxes and our minds, the government passed the Can Spam Act, which took effect in January of 2004. The goal was a spam-free future. Now if only someone would convey this good news to that ex-government official in Nairobi, who keeps asking me to help him with his money transfer.

Of course, this is part of the problem. Some spammers are legitimate, if mis-guided, entrepreneurs, eager to share with us an irresistible opportunity for cheap vitamins and low-cost prescription drugs. On the other hand, many spammers are criminals, who break already existing consumer protection laws with impunity, by hiding outside the US borders to do their dirty work.

For those of us whose CRM strategy includes email contact with customers (and any good CRM strategy should), these illegitimate spammers are an enemy of the first order. One can only hope that the Can Spam Act can clean up the playing field for all of us, by shifting responsibility from the individual states to the federal government, which has far greater resources for enforcement.

Clearly, retailers have a strong interest in keeping the email lines of communica-tion open and spam-free. Email is the preferred contact method among retailers to enlighten customers about new products, services or promotions. More impor-tantly, according to a DoubleClick statistic, E-mail is also the preferred method of communication for 59 percent of consumers. Statistically, email is a win-win! We need the spamming to stop, so that customers continue to feel comfortable providing us with their email address.

Luckily, the federal government also recognizes that we have a legitimate busi-ness interest in emailing our customers. All of the existing statutes and legislation continue to allow us to email those who consent to receive our communications, or those with whom we have a *pre-existing business relationship*. Does that phrase sound familiar? It's the same clause that allows us to work around the Do Not Call Registry. It's also what Customer Relationship Management is all about.

1) **But what constitutes a pre-existing business relationship?**

   The recipient of our email has made a purchase, requested information, responded to a questionnaire or a survey, or had off line contact with us at some time in the last 13 months. (The limit is18 months for the Do Not Call registry). Frankly, if we haven't talked to our customer in 13 months, we probably don't have much of a relationship left.

2) **What constitutes consent?**

   This is almost like dating in high school and college. The judge is looking for the consumer's clear understanding. The recipient of our email must be clearly and fully notified of the collection and use of his or her email address, and have consented prior to such collection and use. This is often called informed consent.

3) **What does it take to comply with the law?**

- Have a pre-existing business relationship, and always gain informed consent before entering into an email communication
- Evaluate your mailing list, and determine the source of the email addresses
- When there's any doubt concerning informed consent, send an email requesting permission to communicate in the future
- Keep a record of the source for each address you add to the list

EXACT TARGET, a legitimate e-mail target marketer processor and the email processor for this newsletter, has provided *Jems*, with invaluable material on the impact of the CAN SPAM Act, the federal legislation, to individuals and marketers.

Suggestions:

If in doubt, please contact your own attorney for their recommendations on the compliance steps necessary for your organization.

1. Include Opt-out in every email
2. Include a valid physical address in every email
3. Avoid misleading subject lines
4. Watch FTC labeling guidelines
5. Maintain a master unsubscribe list for all communications
6. Enforce Opt-out in your organization, requiring compliance in 10 days.

To really go the extra mile, and prove your harmless intentions, consider a double opt-in policy. This let's the customer see how seriously you take the Can Spam Act. It's also more efficient, as it saves you from adding fraudulent emails to a list. Mailing to false addresses increases the number of undeliverable emails, and makes you more susceptible to the "spam trap" that some ISP's have put in place. In the end, subscribers who have opted in twice are less likely to complain. Best of all, your can is covered in the unlikely event of litigation.

Don't be an intruder. Be a guest. We need to keep all lines of communication open—so it's in our interest to protect the consumer from unwanted stalkers. Where's Samuel Jackson when you need him? You thought snakes on a plane were scary? Try spam in your mailbox!

My Suggestion:

    Avoid scaring anyone.

Never wear a mask, and always show them the way out.

(Wk 4: Postal terror [Nightmare on Mail Street])

Has anyone noticed that Halloween is no longer just for kids? In fact, these days there are more grown-ups than children lurking around the streets in costumes (or maybe I just thought those people were in costume.) Instead of finding a tiny ghost and Cinderella knocking at your door, you get a middle-aged couple dressed up as Caesar and Cleopatra, wondering if 1817 Oakwood Drive is "where the party's at?"

So here's a horror story for the grown-ups, guaranteed to send shivers down any retailer's spine:

What if we threw a store party and no one came? What if we had a store promotion and no one responded?

Madness! Mayhem! Mystery! How could this have happened?

Hmm. If our party is on Halloween, and the invitations are delivered on the first of November, we don't have to search for any supernatural explanations. The only ghosts are in the machines, or the people running them.

Read on, for a terrifying tale from the Beyond:

The firm that was contracted to deliver the mail pieces to the Break Bulk Centers delivered one whole palate of mail to the wrong Break Bulk Center. (Did I hear someone scream? It must be the VP of Marketing!)

Just when you thought it was safe … here's another scenario:

Rather than producing all of the mail pieces and shipping them at one time, the production house mailed the pieces as they finished binding them—sending about 50,000 per week. About 70% of the pieces were never mailed. (The horror of it!)

The real horror was that in the old days (a few years ago), we never found out about these kinds of postal delivery problems until:

1) no one showed up at the party …

2) some people showed up from the West side of Manhattan, but nobody came from the East side …

3) plenty of people showed up, and the first thing they mentioned was the late delivery of the invitations …

If only we had known where and when the invitations were being delivered, or not being delivered—we could have done something, before it was too late! If we'd seen the problem in advance, we could have identified it, corrected it, and had the invitations in the customer's hands before the night of the party.

Well, open your candy bags kids, because your kindly neighbor Claude has a treat to share with you. It's called Planet Code Tracking. I know it sounds a little sci-fi. Nevertheless, this is a great new facility developed by USPS a few years ago, with the potential to send an early warning signal for mailing disasters like the ones we've described. The concept is simple. The execution is where the action is.

Here's how it works:

1. An account number is set up for each mailing, like the one we did for our big Halloween bash.

2. That number is converted to a barcode and printed on the mail piece by the mail house.

3. As the mail piece passes thru all the various distribution points, USPS uses its new automation to scan every piece. The information is then sent to the company we've designated to track our mail piece. With the state of technology today, it is almost instantaneous from the scanning to the update by our tracking service.

4. The tracking service, using their own software, keeps track of all of the scans at the various distribution points. More importantly, they make it available to the company doing the mailing, normally with on-line access.

5. The retailer's reports, either on-line or off, will show that all is occurring as expected or may identify some abnormality *before the party starts*.

6. If we're mailing a million pieces, we can literally keep track of each individual piece. The real power of this process is in keeping track of the aggregate. If the vast majority of the mail pieces have not reached a certain stage in a reasonable amount of time, or some smaller geographical area is having a problem, phone calls can be made to track, identify the problem, and redirect the mail.

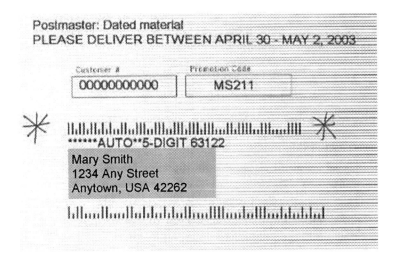

The sample mailing shows how the Planet Code would appear on the mailing label that is printed on the mail piece. The Planet Code is bar-coded, so that it is not readily apparent to the recipient, but it will register with the computer scanning system. Don't worry about the technology. It works.

% of the mailing scanned thru the Postal Service					Party Time
Date-> 27-Dec	28-Dec	29-Dec	30-Dec	31-Dec	1-Jan
NJ 93.7%	94.1%	99.5%	99.5%	99.5%	100.0%
NY 93.9%	93.9%	95.6%	95.7%	97.6%	98.5%
CT 60.8%	79.7%	87.0%	88.7%	93.8%	99.8%
NH 2.1%	10.0%	72.1%	72.8%	93.5%	100.0%
RI 86.8%	93.6%	98.5%	98.5%	100.0%	100.0%
MA 46.9%	83.2%	96.2%	96.5%	98.3%	99.2%
Total 78.2%	92.2%	92.9%	96.7%	99.5%	99.5%

The report above will illustrate the power of the software provided by some of the mailing service companies.

This chart reflects the percentage of the total mailing scanned into the states monitored in the report. If we look only at the "total" line, we might assume all is well a few days before party time (New Year's Eve Party). However, if we look at individual states, we can see that in New Hampshire, only 2.1 percent of the mailing has been delivered by December 27 compared to 46–93 percent for the other states.

With that heads-up, our Marketing Coordinator can get on the phone with the mail house, discover what's happening, and make the necessary changes. Catastrophe averted. As you can see on the chart, by December 31, 93.5 percent of the NH has been delivered.

The same type of report is available from most mailing services at the Bulk Mail Center, Sectional Centers, and zip code level. My army mess sergeant used to say, "Take what you want, but eat what you take." Here, we take what we will use. We can take whatever information is most relevant to our mailing.

Don't let your New Year's Eve party turn into the night of the living dead. Don't let your store become as lonely and abandoned as the proverbial haunted house on the hill. An early alarm system can let us know when things are going wrong, horribly wrong …

Communication breakdowns are the nightmares of CRM. We can't close our eyes, and we can't look away. We're better to face our retail fright night and find solutions—fast.

My Suggestion:

   If you haven't used Planet Coding, step into the future.

Spot your problems before, not after, the damage is done.

Chapter XI

November—Thanks for shopping. Come back soon.

(Wk 1: "Thank you"—the original warm fuzzy)

When was the last time we sent that message on something other than the bottom of a sales receipt? Especially when it comes to our best customers, it might not be such a bad thing to **communicate**. After all, these are the people giving us the vast majority of our sales, and almost all of our profits. A little gratitude would be appropriate.

It would also be important to give the customer some encouragement for a return visit. This is what customer retention is all about—and these are the exact customers we need to retain. Whatever we can do to get these particular customers back in the store, sooner rather than later, is well worth our money and effort.

Nevertheless, over the years, I've worked with retail CFO's who say: *"We don't have to do anything special for the best customers. We already know they like us. They're going to repurchase anyway. Why would we spend money on them?"* Of course, that's not <u>our</u> CFO. These are bean counters with no understanding of human nature.

I recently had a client with a visionary head of marketing, who wanted to surprise her best customers and thank them at the same time. She decided to test the water with her top 50,000 patrons, sending them a $25 gift certificate good for one month—no minimum purchase, no purchase threshold, no other strings attached. This was a truly tangible way to say thank you. And it was indeed a surprise, as the customers had no expectation of receiving the offer.

That surprise element is important. To do something like this too often will eliminate the element of surprise, and could "train" our customers to wait for the offer.

Wouldn't you know the client's CFO did not share the marketing officer's enthusiasm for a small show of customer appreciation? He knew what was going to happen:

"They'll come in, find $25 worth of merchandise they were going to buy anyway, and plunk down the gift certificate and leave having spent only $25. We'll have a bunch of goose eggs to show for our effort."

Finally, the Chief Marketing Officer prevailed, but only by putting her reputation on the line. The results would be unveiled by the CMO at the next Executive Committee Meeting.

Can you stand the suspense?

Fast forward to one month later: the results were in!

- About half of the best customers took advantage of the offer.
- The average spent on a monthly basis for those who took advantage of the offer dropped about $25 (no big surprise).
- The sales for the responders had a reduced margin of $625,000 compared to a normal month for these responders.

BUT there was an **increase of over $3,000,000 in margin** for that month over those "best customers" who did not respond.

Maybe there's something in this "thank you" thing, after all. Maybe letting our best customers know we appreciate them is actually good business. Who knew?

Let's try using a little of that thing we talked about a couple of weeks ago: common sense. One way to retain our top customers is by telling them "thanks" every now and then. One way to build our business is by getting our best customers to come back to the store and shop again. Anything that does both can't be all bad.

My Suggestion:

Don't take the best customers for granted.

Make a gesture that clearly tells them how much you appreciate their continued patronage. Then, be sure that gesture brings them back into the store to shop. You'll have done something nice for your customer, yourself, and your bottom line.

(Wk 2: Hugs even to the "returner")

Someone said once that the greatest expression of gratitude is to give something back in return. Whoever said that wasn't in retail. No one likes a "returner (someone who returns merchandise to the store)."

That's why, back when I was a retailer, we made the return process as onerous as possible, hoping that customers would not want the bother of bringing merchandise back. Go over to the special desk, the one with the line of twenty-five people and one clerk. Prove to the clerk who you are. Now prove to the clerk that you bought the merchandise. It's true—you're holding it in your hand. But maybe you found it on the street …

In a recent article in the New York Post, entitled "You Buy It, You Keep It", journalist Rich Calder describes retailers who've gone even one step further. They've developed a new facility to track customers who return merchandise. The theory is that when these "returners" reach a certain threshold, they'll be shut down. "No Returns For You!!" as Seinfeld's Soup Nazi might say. What a great idea. Returns are bad. Therefore "returners" must be bad. The sooner we can identify one, the sooner we can stop the other.

A long time friend of mine, a top executive at high-end menswear retailer, had an encounter with someone from the store's operations department, who told him: "We've got this guy who's returned about $12,000 of merchandise in the last twelve months. Something's got to be done!" "You better believe it", thought my friend, his mind immediately conjuring up the possibility of physical torture, blistering nasty-gram correspondences, or some form of public humiliation.

But not too long before, my friend had read an obscure article in a newsletter by some CRM nut—one of those warm and fuzzy types always telling you to hug your customers. Just as an exercise, my friend decided to run a report on this customer's total sales, returns and net spend for the last twelve months. Guess what he found?

This customer had purchased $56,000 worth of product. Indeed, he had returned $12,000 of it. Nevertheless, that left a net purchase for the year of $44,000. It turns out that this returner was not just any slug off the street. This was one of the company's best customers.

So did my friend take away this customer's return privileges anyway? No. Did he send him a scathing diatribe telling him to take his returns and his future business elsewhere? Not exactly.

My friend sent the customer a letter, thanking him for being one of the company's best customers, and encouraging him to come back and shop again soon.

WAIT A SECOND! HOLD THE PRESSES! WHAT JUST HAPPENED HERE?!?

Did someone just reward a "returner"? Am I saying that "returners" are good?!

No. I'm saying that "returners" are the best. In fact, the BEST customers almost always have the highest rate of returns. Below, you'll find the purchase segmentation for spring 2004, with the D-R-O-P segmentation we've discussed previously (Diamond, Ruby, Opal and Pearl). The next chart reflects the purchase history of those customers who had a return during spring 2004.

All Spring, 2004 Buyers					
Monetary Segment	Cust Count	% of Total	Lifetime Purchases	% of Total	Avg Spend
Diamond	50,200	12.9%	$ 10,989,741	31.6%	$ 218.92
Ruby	63,778	16.4%	$ 7,515,432	21.6%	$ 117.84
Opal	187,686	48.2%	$ 13,115,242	37.7%	$ 69.88
Pearl	87,859	22.6%	$ 3,197,985	9.2%	$ 36.40
Total	389,523		$ 34,818,400		$ 89.39

Spring, 2004 Buyers who returned mdse during Spring, 2004					
Diamond	7,769	2.0%	$ (649,308)	-1.9%	$ (83.58)
Ruby	6,023	1.5%	$ (424,487)	-1.2%	$ (70.48)
Opal	13,679	3.5%	$ (864,857)	-2.5%	$ (63.23)
Pearl	9,864	2.5%	$ (559,188)	-1.6%	$ (56.69)
Total	37,335		$ (2,497,840)		$ (66.90)

Spring, 2004 Net Sales for Spring, 2004 Returners					
Diamond	7,769	2.0%	$ 1,830,217	5.3%	$ 235.58
Ruby	6,023	1.5%	$ 703,292	2.0%	$ 116.77
Opal	13,679	3.5%	$ 915,438	2.6%	$ 66.92
Pearl	9,864	2.5%	$ 318,822	0.9%	$ 32.32
Total	37,335		$ 3,767,769		$ 100.92

As we can see, the best customers, the Diamonds, did indeed have the highest average returns. Would we want to punish our best customers?

At the bottom of the chart, we can see net purchases for those who had a return during the spring season. Here again, the average net spend by returners is $100.92, in comparison to $89.39 for other customers who had no returns. Are we sure we want to punish our best customers?

The next chart pulls out only the best customers (a veritable treasure trove of Diamonds and Rubies). Together, this group makes up 29 percent of the spring customer population, and produces 53 percent of the business.

Diamond/Ruby (Best) Customers who bought and returned					
	Cust Count	% of Total	Lifetime Purchases	% of Total	Avg Spend
Total Net Sales	113,978	29.3%	18,505,173	53.1%	$ 336.76
Buyers (No Returns)	100,186	25.7%	15,971,664	45.9%	$ 159.42
Returners (Net Sales)	13,792	3.5%	2,533,509	7.3%	$ 352.35

These "top" customers can be segmented further into two groups:

1. **Those customers who bought merchandise and did not return any of it.** This group represents 28 percent of the "buy it and keep it" population and 51 percent of the "buy and keep it" dollars. Their average net spend is $159.42. These are good guys. We won't kick them out of bed.

2. **Those customers who purchased merchandise, but (God forbid) returned some of it.** They represent 27 percent of the "returner" population, and 67 percent of the "returner" dollars. Their average net spend is $183.69. That's $124 higher than the "buy it and keep it" crowd. There's no doubt about it. "Returners" are, quite literally, a retailer's best friends.

So what should we do about the "problem" of returns, then? Should we go ahead and fire off a letter anyway? I think so. I'm with my friend, the menswear executive. I'd send the "returners" a letter to say "thanks for your business" and encourage them to come back soon—even if it's to make a return.

My Suggestion:

Treat people making returns as if they're your very best customers.

They are. Keep the return process as simple and easy as possible. Remember, if the customer doesn't feel comfortable enough to return merchandise, he or she won't feel comfortable enough to make a future purchase at your store.

(Wk 3: Come back soon—SOON, got it?)

Thanks for Shopping. Come Back Soon.

It's good to say thanks. It's good to keep them coming back for more. But it's the little word at the end of the phrase that makes it all work:

Come Back *Soon.*

The fact is: if they don't come back soon, they're probably not coming back at all. Effective customer retention depends on timing. The longer we wait to get started, the harder it is to accomplish.

Customer retention is a term with a thousand definitions. Some retailers have traditionally defined it as "the percentage of buyers who repurchase from one year to the next." Do you remember our old definition?

The Customer Retention Rate is the percentage of customers who make 2 or more purchases within 6 months.

That's a much more accurate yardstick by which to measure our success in retention. But here's how another retailer defined the term. This retailer has a very high retention rate of 67.1 percent. Clearly then, this way of looking at the subject can yield its own rewards:

The Customer Retention Rate is the percentage of buyers who repurchase from one season to the next.

In other words, a customer is retained if, having purchased anytime during the spring season, and he or she then repurchases at any time during the fall season. Seems simple enough.

Here's the important bit:

> **We won't know until the end of the fall season what our retention rate is from the spring.**

If the spring season is February thru July, then by August 1, we can identify all of our spring season customers. But did they all purchase in July? Of course not. Do we think that those whose last purchase was in February/March/April will be retained at the same rate as the buyer whose last purchase was in July? No, again.

Do we think all tiers have the same retention rate by month of last purchase? Once again, negative.

| $ Segment | Spring, 2002 Buyers | | | | |
| | Customers Active Prior to Spring, 2002 | | | | |
	Cust Count	% of Total	Purchases	% of Total	Avg Spend
Tier 1	26,900	8.5%	$ 40,000,000	40.0%	$ 1,487
Tier 2	60,700	19.1%	$ 29,000,000	29.0%	$ 478
Tier 3	110,000	34.6%	$ 23,000,000	23.0%	$ 209
Tier 4	120,000	37.8%	$ 8,000,000	8.0%	$ 67
Total	317,600		$ 100,000,000		$ 315

| $ Segment | Spring, 2002 Buyers Retained into Fall, 2002 | | | | |
| | Customers Active Prior to Spring, 2002 | | | | |
	Cust Count	Retain Rate	Purchases	Retain Rate	Avg Spend
Tier 1	22,000	81.8%	$ 32,000,000	80.0%	$ 1,455
Tier 2	50,000	82.4%	$ 20,000,000	69.0%	$ 400
Tier 3	74,000	67.3%	$ 21,000,000	91.3%	$ 284
Tier 4	67,000	55.8%	$ 12,000,000	150.0%	$ 179
Total	213,000	67.1%	$ 85,000,000	85.0%	$ 399

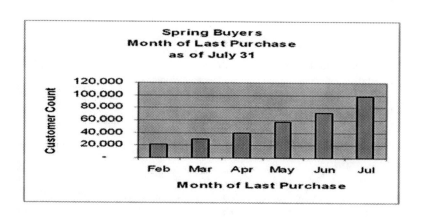

The chart above reflects 317,600 spring buyers, distributed as to the month of their last purchase, at the end of the spring season. Is anyone surprised that the retention rate diminishes, as we go from right to left on the chart? Not really. But *how much* does retention diminish, as the time from the last purchase increases?

Month Of Last Purch.	Spring Buyer	Purchased Again in Fall	Retention Rate
Feb	21,282	4,603	21.6%
Mar	30,177	13,878	46.0%
Apr	39,221	22,371	57.0%
May	57,022	36,732	64.4%
Jun	71,815	52,788	73.5%
Jul	98,081	82,627	84.2%
Total		213,000	67.1%

The problem with this breakdown is that the message can only be seen in retrospect. If retention is measured from season to season, we wouldn't know that 78.4 percent of our February purchasers were not retained, until the fall season is over. By the time we see it, it's too late. If we wait until fall is over, our chances of getting the customer to ever repurchase again will have diminished to nearly zero.

How much better would it be if toward the end of the spring season, we identified our spring customers by the month of their last purchase during the season? Then, we could immediately focus our retention efforts on those customers, just as the spring season was closing—and right when our efforts would be most effective. That way, we could improve our retention *before* the fall season ends.

This very short time horizon gives our company the ability to better monitor and manage retention for the various customer segments. As soon as retention begins to sag in one segment or another, we can make quick adjustments to get back on track. Bad news isn't so bad when we still have time to make it better.

My Suggestion:

> **When it comes to measuring retention, keep the timeframe tight, to get a head start, rather than hindsight.**

Try measuring retention on a seasonal or a quarterly basis. This will allow you to take action before the season ends, to improve your retention results.

(Wk 4: Incentives to come back)

I remember back when I was in the Army (yes, in the twentieth century), we would be sent on long, forced marches to test our endurance. The thing that really made these activities fun was near the end of the course, when those who were leading the march would start adding obstacles—as if a 10-mile forced march wasn't obstacle enough.

Obviously, we were being tested. The leaders wanted to see who could get over the obstacle and continue. The closer to the finish line a soldier got, the more difficult the obstacle became, and fewer and fewer soldiers were able to surmount it.

Strangely enough, we do the same thing in the retail industry. Best of all, we call it a "gift" or a "reward". Even the military didn't have the chutzpah to try that.

Think about it:

Some offer is made to our customers, a gift certificate or special discount, to entice them to return to the store and shop. It's what we've been talking about all month: "Thanks For Shopping. Come Back Soon." But instead of simply offering a gift that expresses our gratitude, we put an obstacle in place that the customer must hurdle over. Rather than offer a reward of $25 with no restrictions, we include a minimum purchase requirement.

Remember our CMO who wanted to thank her best customers? She immediately ran into objections from the CFO, who thought it sounded more like a special grand giveaway. He was convinced the recipients of the gift would come in, spend their $25 and leave.

Fair enough. After all, we do have to protect the business. What are the ramifications of eliminating the threshold, or obstacle? What happened with this event?

To start with, it's clear that no threshold means more people will respond. In the Army's forced march, fewer obstacles will result in more people at the finish line. A retailer who eliminates the purchase requirement will see more customers at the cash wrap. There's not much doubt about this. By eliminating the threshold, we can better persuade both the regular customer and the best customer to respond.

But is it worth it? Will those customers who respond to the no threshold offer, *but who would not respond to an offer with a minimum purchase*, shop at profitable rate? Let's go back to our event, and see:

- About half of the best customers took advantage of the offer.
- The average spent on a monthly basis for those who took advantage of the offer dropped about $25 (no big surprise).
- The sales for the responders had a reduced margin of $625,000 compared to a normal month for these responders.

BUT there was **an increase of over $3,000,000** in margin in June over those best customers who did not respond.

Obviously, the event itself was quite successful. But is that the end of it? Does this breakdown of results tell the full story?

There's a Jewish word, *mitzvah*, which translates roughly as "one good deed begets another". (My apologies to my Jewish friends for what's lost in the translation). It's worth keeping in mind, especially when we're thanking our best customers. Let's look at the bigger picture:

We normalized the responders with the non-responders to create a group of equal quantity. Then, we tracked each group backwards for each of 3 preceding months. This gave us a base performance for comparison purposes, prior to the June event. After the event, we then tracked each group for the next 3 months.

Sometimes, nice guys finish first. It turns out that the difference between the two groups increased considerably from the base comparison before the event. In fact, the difference in the monthly purchase rate went up over one-third. The incremental sales over those 3 months was more than 2 million dollars, with a small reduced margin, as the best customers took advantage of the special offers at a higher rate than the control group.

My mom used to say, "Give a gift and you will get a gift." Not a bad thing to think about, especially as we begin that season of giving and receiving.

My Suggestion:

   Try giving a gift.

It's nice. You'll like it. Your customers will like it. And ultimately, it will have a positive effect on your bottom line.

Happy Thanksgiving! See you at the mall on Friday …

Chapter XII

December—Gifts That Keep on Giving

(Wk 1: Rushing through the season)

Speaking of gifts, as we were last week, I hope you've joined the rest of the country in starting your holiday shopping. Just for the record: I'm a 42 Regular; I like my sweaters in blue, and my sports cars in red. You did remember to get something for kindly Uncle Claude, didn't you? He got something for you …

With best wishes for a fruitful holiday, and a bountiful new year, I give you:

Gifts That Keep On Giving

If you've been in retail for long, you know that this is not the month for grand themes, or brave new ideas. In December, we stack 'em high and let 'em fly. If you work in a store, put this book down and go help someone. You can catch up in January. If you work in the corporate office, try not to get in the way. Now is not the time to call the stores and roll out your exciting new program. Make a note, and take it up when the smoke clears.

So, to wind up the year's *Jems*, we're going to keep it simple. I want to give you 5 fundamental ideas that you can use today, and throughout the New Year. Consider them my present to you.

Let's start with a happy story. We'll hope it's being reenacted in your store right now:

A few days ago, my wife and I visited a Chico's store that recently opened in Melbourne, Florida. When it comes to my own personal financial picture, this opening is probably the worst news I could hope to receive (postponing any hopes of retirement for another decade). Still, I have to acknowledge that the associate who handled our transaction was a CRM man's dream. She seemed to be as interested in the customer as she was in the product. Even better, she was focused on getting the information right, which is the surest way to my heart.

Since Chico's has a card-based loyalty program, she asked if we had our Passport Card. "Of course," was the answer. Then, she asked if the information was still correct. We confirmed the address. But when it came to the phone number, we realized that the number had changed. She made the correction immediately.

This was not a quiet day in the store. Chico's had plenty of customers. Still, this associate took the time to get things right. She handled each customer and the gathering of the customer information as if it were just as important as insuring that the product was properly rung up on the register. In her mind, anything less than 100 percent capture rate with "all information correct" would have been a failure.

At this time of year, with our stores full of customers new and old, what could be as valuable as an associate focused on obtaining the information we need for effective CRM? Now is the time we should be growing our database. The one thing we can't afford is customer shrinkage.

Customer what?

This isn't the kind of shrinkage we get from washing cotton in hot water. This is "the incredible shrinking customer" who goes from 'Big Spender' to the 'Invisible Man' in less time than it takes to say, "Can I confirm your address?" Shrinkage occurs when less than 100 percent of the transactions in the store are posted to a valid, mail-able, customer record. If we don't have what we need to **communicate**, then we didn't capture the customer. Honey, I shrunk the business!

We'll always have some customer shrinkage. Some customers will never give their name and address. Still, it's up to us to do all we can to reduce this reluctance, through loyalty programs, and a relentless emphasis on training for the associates in the stores. The failure to obtain information more often stems from an employee's reluctance to ask for it, than from a customer's reluctance to provide it. We must train, train, and retrain.

It helps to know what we're looking for, and where we can spot it. The following chart separates our customer shrinkage into three specific areas:

1,061,424	Annual Transactions
965,896	Some customer information captured
91.0%	Reported Capture Rate
95,528	Uncaptured Transactions
9.0%	**A-Customer Shrinkage**
84,914	Address validation software captured
8.0%	**B-Customer Shrinkage**
127,371	Unmailable addresses
12.0%	**C-Customer Shrinkage**

To begin, we can see that the client has 9 percent customer shrinkage attributable directly to customers who are reluctant to provide their names and addresses. Actually, this is quite low for most retailers. This particular client has a very interactive retail format. Other formats will have considerably higher shrinkage in this area.

An additional 8 percent shrinkage occurs when the records are processed by address verification/validation software. If this processing occurs after polling, the customer records may be identified as incorrect, but no correction can occur because the customer is no longer in the store.

Happily, this source of shrinkage is largely preventable. There are PC software packages available that validate the entry of the data at point of sale. This allows the error to be caught immediately, before the customer leaves the store.

We saved the biggest problem for last, and it leads right back to my friend at Chico's. Most customer shrinkage is due to invalid entry by the associate. Some errors are accidental; some are not. For associates tired of asking the customer for his or her address, one favorite trick is to enter instead the address of the store. This will get the transaction by most CRM software. Of course, it will be discovered once the information gets back to the database. But by then, the damage is done. The customer has left the building.

It all comes down to little mistakes that add up to big shrink. Like inventory shrinkage, the largest portion of customer shrinkage results from an associate who fails to pay attention to details, or intentionally enters incorrect information. Not everyone has the dedication of the Chico's superstar my wife and I met last week.

On the plus side, customer shrinkage, like inventory shrinkage, can be controlled.

Tis the season to grow our business, not shrink it. Certainly, we wouldn't accept 29 percent inventory shrinkage. Neither should we accept that kind of sloppiness when it comes to customer shrinkage. Once we have these customers in our database, the CRM possibilities are endless. Getting them in there correctly is a gift that keeps on giving ...

My Suggestion:

   Don't let your database dwindle.

Train and train again, to help associates persuade that 9 percent of reluctant customers to provide the necessary information. Use additional POS software to catch the 8 percent of invalid addresses, before the customer gets away. Institute controls for reporting and monitoring shrinkage, and identify problems quickly at the store and associate levels to cut the 12 percent "bad information" figure down to size.

(Wk 2: Fruitcake—it's NOT nutty!)

"Hello? Hello? Is this the party to whom I am speaking?"

Phoning our best customers is probably the most effective strategy in our entire CRM playbook. It's quick, low-cost, and as personal as we can hope to get. But not every retailer gets it right. Sometimes the greatest gift is being saved from our own great ideas.

Here's a CRM program I came across recently:

In order to help and encourage their store personnel to phone the best customers, this retailer's marketing department agreed to print out a listing of all the customers for the assigned store on a quarterly basis. This listing averaged 7,200 customers and 144 pages per store. The chart below reflects the high level statistics on a quarterly basis.

Customer listings going to the stores

1,800,000	Customers on the database
250	# of Stores
7,200	Average count of customers per store
144	Average number of pages per store

What do you think? I call this a fruitcake idea. It's like one of those traditional fruitcakes that get passed around at the holidays. It looks pretty good from the outside. But once you bite into it, you change your mind. Just like the fruitcake, this idea is nothing but nuts.

Straight from the corporate office comes this simple report, with the customer number, name, address, city, state, zip code, and phone number (if there were one on file). But has anyone considered:

Which of these customers should get called and which should not?

What criteria would be used to determine who gets called? Should they be called in alphabetical order? Are the phone numbers still good?

What about the Do Not Call legislation? Which customers have no relationship with the store in the last 18 months?

Which customers are in the store's trade area?

What is the store's trade area?

What do we talk about with the customer every three months, assuming we actually make the calls?

Certainly, we want our store personnel to call our best customers. This is the first step in building a relationship, upon which so many of our CRM efforts depend. But do we really think the stores should spend 360 hours every three months, calling their customers? That's 3 minutes per call, multiplied by 7200 customers.

This is not the way to conduct a phone campaign. Let's use what we've learned of CRM to turn this idea from fruitcake to fruitful. We need to:

1)   Focus the efforts of the store personnel where we can get the biggest bang for the buck.

2)   Insure that the information on the listing is correct, meaningful and timely.

Here, then, is your gift for the second week of the holiday season: a money-saving, paper-reducing, results-boosting guide to building relationships by calling your best customers. You'll thank me in the morning.

Start by defining a "Best Customer". Above all else, these are the folks we *must* call. It's not absolute, but in most cases, past purchase performance points toward future purchase performance. So let's reach into the database and narrow down this definition.

It's not hard to start. If they don't spend a lot of money in the store, they're not a "Best Customer". Monetary spending is a very important metric; to qualify; these should be people whose purchase history puts them in the top 20 percent of our customers.

We should also ask, "What have you done for us lately?" Previously, we defined a "Best Customer" as one who had purchased in the last 6 months. Retailers vary on this, with some having reverse horizons as short as 3 months, and others going as long as 12 months.

Even if we stick with the long view, at 12 months, this recency metric has the added benefit of eliminating the possibility for violating the Do Not Call legislation. This way, we won't phone anyone with whom we've been out of touch for more than 18 months.

Finally, we should be careful about ignoring the boy next door. Proximity is another consideration in defining our "best customer". Remember our store trade area? That's the geography around the store that makes up about 80 percent of our customer base. Our best customers live there, right in our backyard.

Using these more precise measurements, the chart below reflect the count of our "Best Customers", as we've defined them:

Previous customer listings going to the stores

1,800,000	Customers on the database
250	# of Stores
7,200	Average count of customers per store
144	Average number of pages per store

New-Quarterly Listing of Best Customers going to the stores

250,000	Top customers for the last 6 months
14%	% of customer base
62%	% of purchases coming form top 14% of customer base
250	# of stores
1,000	Average count of Best Customers per store
20	Average number of pages per store

These criteria will help us reduce the customer listing to 250,000 out of 1.8 million. In fact, about 14 percent of the customer base has spent over $200 in the last 6 months and live within the store's trade area. This brings the average count per store from 7,200 names to be called, to just 1,000 names per store. We'll hear no complaints from the store personnel there.

Once we've found our Best Customer, we're just starting the winnowing process. Let's use those handy computers in our office, and try ranking the customers in descending dollars to allow associates to call their *best* Customer first. Even among the best, some are better than others.

With this ranking, the associates will be encouraged to call the best customers first, just in case they don't get all the calls made before the next quarterly report. We could even sort the listing by assigned associate (that is, the one who has worked most often with the customer), and then move on to ranking by dollar amount.

But WAIT! There's more! (Now I sound like a game show host.) Since the computer knows all of the customer's purchases over the last 6 months, we can print one row for each department, vendor, and/or class, showing the units and dollar purchased. *Voila'.* We've just solved another problem. We've given the associate something to talk about with his or her best customer.

That is, if he or she can reach the customer ...

How comfortable are we with the accuracy of the phone number itself? We can't afford to have the associate wasting time calling a number that's been changed or disconnected. We really can't afford to have the associate unknowingly call a cell phone, especially at the wrong time!

Before sending out this list of names and numbers to the stores, we *must* do a phone verify/append. This is not optional. If we are asking store associates or a call center to do outbound calling, then we need to:

- Verify that the phone number is correct for the customer at the address given.
- Replace any incorrect or missing numbers with a valid phone number.
- Blank the phone number field, if no valid number is available. This record should not be sent to the store.

It's not enough to do the calling. We have to make it cost effective. That's what a phone verify/append is all about. The data below is from a case study with AccuData (out of Fort Myers, FL).

Through this particular verify/append, we were able to weed out 62,500 customers for whom we had a bad telephone number. Had we not removed these names, we would have spent 3 minutes of wasted time for each customer, along with wasted salary. If the average associate makes 10 dollars per hour, we just saved $31,250.

Cost of the telephone verify/append: Less than $1000. *Priceless.*

My Suggestion:

Nothing is more effective than a phone call.

You can call all of the people some of the time. You can call some of the people all of the time. You can't call all of the people all of the time. Nothing's more effective than a phone call, if you do it right. Knowing who to call, and how, is another gift that keeps on giving.

(Wk 3: Hiding the gifts)

Hello. Where's the store?

You sent me this pretty postcard, offering me $25 off my next purchase. But **where is the store?**

The postcard came in an expensive package, telling me about your new store. Nice. **But where is the store?**

I also received a beautiful catalog with all the pretty, new merchandise in it. But **where the heck is the store?**

Then I had an email from you, inviting me to come in. **But where is your blasted store?**

I moved, but the post office forwarded your mail piece to me, at my new address. BUT WHERE THE HECK IS YOUR STORE!?!

Yes, it's true. I did see the instruction to call the 800 number, or go to the web to find the store nearest me. I wasn't actually looking for a research project. If you can't tell me where the store is, I'm not going to take my valuable time to look it up.

It seems simple. When we're trying to persuade prospects to come and visit our store for the first time, wouldn't it be wise to make the experience as easy as possible? Let's start by telling them where the store is.

Some retailers seem to believe that "if you build it, they will come." Maybe. But first, we have to tell them where it is. We don't ask them to call for information or look it up on the web. We can just tell them. Have we not bothered to set up a process for determining the store nearest to our customer's home?

Computers (those big metal boxes in the back office) can be used to identify the store to which we want to invite our prospect. It's amazing what these machines can do. All we have to do is identify which stores customers in a specific geographical area are currently patronizing. Using that information, another program can determine in which geography our prospect lives. The probability is very, very high that the prospect will want to go to the store that's been designated for that area. Why would someone not go to the store nearest his or her home?

Using this same technology, we can also remind our current customers of the location of the nearest store. Sure, they've been there before. I've been to Los Angeles before—but when I go back, I bring a map. People forget. We go to the store every day for work. On the other hand, the customer may visit us once a year, when they need what we're selling. Let's help them out. We can give them a hint where we are.

And don't forget about those movers and shakers. NCOA processing will identify between 15–20 percent of our file that moves every year. These people are not going to go out on a search mission on our behalf. Once we know they've moved, and where they've gone, let's tell them where the nearest store is.

Here's how to do it:

We'll start by assuming that we have one store, and are able to determine in which zip codes our customers live. The chart below reflects a very simple spreadsheet, counting the customers by zip code, then sorted in a descending count. Notice that this particular store has 1,458 customers in their top zip code, accounting for 24.1 percent of their customer base. Surprise, surprise. The store is located in that zip code. I told you so, remember? The store is always located in the top zip code. Proximity to the store is the second biggest indicator of customer response.

Any consumer living in these top zip codes can be told where the nearest store is.

Store Trade Area Definition						
	Customers			Sales		
Zip Code	Count	% of Store	Accum	Sales	% of Store	Accum
1 10024	1,458	24.10%	24.10%	$192,866	26.30%	26.30%
2 10025	677	11.20%	35.30%	$95,678	13.10%	39.40%
3 10023	354	5.90%	41.20%	$45,270	6.20%	45.60%
4 10021	143	2.40%	43.50%	$25,280	3.50%	49.00%
5 10028	122	2.00%	45.60%	$14,436	2.00%	51.00%
6 10128	119	2.00%	47.50%	$15,613	2.10%	53.20%
7 10019	59	1.00%	48.50%	$7,198	1.00%	54.10%
8 10027	54	0.90%	49.40%	$8,495	1.20%	55.30%
9 10463	50	0.80%	50.20%	$5,849	0.80%	56.10%
10 10011	43	0.70%	50.90%	$5,101	0.70%	56.80%
11 6830	39	0.60%	51.60%	$2,928	0.40%	57.20%
12 10014	33	0.50%	52.10%	$2,507	0.30%	57.50%
13 10033	33	0.50%	52.70%	$2,892	0.40%	57.90%
14 10016	32	0.50%	53.20%	$5,036	0.70%	58.60%
15 10003	29	0.50%	53.70%	$3,316	0.50%	59.10%

If we are communicating with a customer in one of these zip codes, we should tell him or her the location of the store using either a map, or a verbal explanation that the customer can understand ("intersection of Route 3 and Route 17, next to Giant Stadium"). Remember, it probably was a long time ago when I was in the store.

"But these customers live in the area. Everyone who lives around here knows us and where our store is. We're a landmark. They can't miss it."

I've learned that whenever someone gives me directions that end with "you can't miss it", I should add an extra hour of travel time, for when I miss it. Don't assume the customer can find us. After all, there are competitors between the customer's home and our location. The customer could just stop there and make the purchase. Perhaps that's what the customer has been doing. If he or she lives in the 20th ranked zip code, and we haven't seen him or her in a year, we can assume that the customer has not been waiting on our spiffy postcard to go shopping.

If we're mailing to customers outside of these 15 zip codes, we'll need to go with the second best option, which is actually not very good at all. We'll print that awful default line: "Call this 800 number to find the store nearest you." Just what every customer needs—another wasted minute of time.

GOTCHA! We wouldn't do this, because we wouldn't be mailing to these customers at all. Why would we mail to customers outside our Store Trade Area? We know that the response to our mailing is correlated to proximity. See how much these "*Jems*" have taught us?

Even if we have multiple stores in a market, with overlapping Store Trade Areas, we can still avoid the dreaded 800 number option. Instead, we can prepare a spreadsheet (a table). Let's call it Zip Code Assignment Table, where each zip code is assigned to the store that has the most customers in that zip code. If we wish, we can then assign a secondary store to that same zip code, which will be the store with the second-most customers in that area. We could carry that on to the third or fourth as well, but let's not go whacko.

We should set an arbitrary threshold count; if no second store has more than the threshold count, then only one store address would appear on the mail piece. Only if no store meets the threshold count would we go with the default message.

We can then take this Zip Code Assignment Table to the mail house. They will read the address label and key off of the zip code. If a zip code is in the Assignment Table, the mail house will print a map of the primary store, and the secondary store (if one exists). If there is no store that meets the threshold for a particular zip code in the Zip Code Assignment Table, then the default line will appear: "Call this 800 number to find the store nearest you".

This time you caught it, didn't you? We shouldn't be mailing to someone in a zip code that doesn't meet the threshold count for assignment of a store. The statistics tell us that we're never going to see this person. The best we could hope for is a catalog or internet sale.

As a child, I always preferred Santa Claus to the Easter Bunny. With Santa, you knew where the gifts were going to be. You just headed for the big tree in the living room. The Easter Bunny liked to hide the basket.

Let's not hide the basket. For a gift that keeps on giving, let's set up programs for telling our prospects and our customers exactly where they can find us.

My Suggestion:

In all your communications with the customer, tell them where the nearest store is.

No mailing is complete without something that tells the prospect or the customer WHERE WE ARE. Use a Zip Code Assignment Table to identify the appropriate stores in the trade area, and then provide a map or directions to the primary and, if necessary, secondary store. Avoid that default line with the 800 number. If the customer isn't close enough to have a store assigned, they won't be coming in anyway.

(Wk 4: Good things DO come in small packages)

Like most children, I always assumed that the biggest package under the tree must contain the best gift. In this area, and it's not the only one, women often catch on faster than men. Girls seem to have an intuitive understanding that very valuable things sometimes come in smaller boxes. Note the difference in reaction to a small blue Tiffany's box, and a fishing-pole size package from Big Jim's Bait and Tackle. This week's gift is a little one—and that's a good thing.

The fact is there's more to mastering CRM in retail than large direct mail events sent to every address on file. These events will always be the centerpiece to our CRM program, as they have the potential to drive millions of dollars worth of business to the stores. But it's smaller, niche events that truly build and maintain relationships with our customers. They generate a much higher response rate, and an enormous return on investment, because they carry a specific message for the targeted customer.

Even better, niche marketing events allow us to **communicate** with our customers without conditioning the customer to expect a discount or markdowns. They give us a reason to be in touch, beyond simple cost savings.

With the idea that good things come in small packages, we've asked our friend, *Christine Spigai, President of On the Mark Communications,* to list a few niche marketing efforts that she has helped manage and implement over the last several years.

Here's Christine's list:

Thank You Gifts—

> Thank your best customers with a scarf, accessory, fragrance or other small item that is not generally available. What a nice way to thank high spenders during the holiday season! You can send this gift to their home in special packaging or invite the customer into the store to receive their gift—no strings attached.

Trunk Show/Preview Invitations—

> Send your best customers an exclusive invitation to trunk shows and fashion preview parties. These shows may be held outside of regular store hours or on weekends to convey a sense of exclusivity.

"Design Your Own" Events—

Give your top-tier customers a sneak, "behind-the-scene" peek to learn what goes into designing and manufacturing particular apparel or accessories. Invite them to custom design a shoe, scarf or other accessory by selecting material, size, color, etc. during these exclusive workshops.

Workshops and Demos—

Teach your best customers "tips from the pros." Invite them to participate in an in-store fashion workshop to learn various makeup or fashion tips and trends. Or invite best customers to participate in free demonstrations, samplings, or seminars.

Secret Savings—

Secret "scratch-off" invitations are successful for all types of retailers—from high-end apparel to furniture. In what really amounts to a game of chance, this invitation invites customers to enjoy special savings, dollars or gifts when they make a purchase. It generally works best if customers are asked to reveal the "secret" at the time of purchase and not beforehand.

Bring a Friend—

A great way to gain new customers is through a "bring-a-friend" promotion where both are invited to enjoy exclusive savings. Friends usually "look alike" demographically, so this is an inexpensive way to introduce qualified prospects to your stores.

Holiday Thanks—

Send your best customers holiday thank-you greetings around Thanksgiving or winter holidays. Design limited edition cards exclusively for this communication, making customers look forward to receiving them each year.

Reactivation—

Identify and **communicate** with high-spending customers who have not recently shopped at your stores. Reactivation incentives must be stronger than general promotions in order to motivate an inactive customer to become active again.

Birthday Wishes—

Collect the birth month of your customers. It's a great idea to send birthday wishes and an invitation to visit their favorite store.

Product-specific Invitations—

Knowing the specific items purchased by your customers allows for product-specific marketing communications. Invite customers to come in for a special preview of new arrivals, according to their product preferences.

New Movers—

Identify customers who have relocated from one store market area to another and send a communication inviting them to the store nearest them. Don't forget the map, showing where the store is! You better include a reward for going to the store as well.

Buy Now, Save Later—

This promotion is a terrific way to move sale merchandise without having to reduce already low margins. When a customer makes a purchase "now", meeting a certain dollar threshold, you reward them with a savings certificate to be used "later"—at a time when full-priced merchandise is plentiful and margins are higher.

Charity Events—

Partner with a charity, to which your customers can donate old clothing, shoes, books, or CD's. In New York City, for example, there are organizations that accept second-hand suits and business attire to help the less fortunate "dress for success" on their next job interview. In exchange for the customers' donations, you can reward them with a savings on their next suit purchase, etc.

Wow. That's 13 gifts in one tiny box. No wonder we call these things *Jems*.

Take advantage of these clever marketing ideas. Used correctly, they'll be gifts that go on giving throughout the year.

Again, thanks, to *Christine Spigai, of On the Mark Communications*, for her input.

My Suggestion:

Do it all.

Use the big, direct mail events as the anchors in your CRM strategy. These will impact large segments of your customer base, and hopefully, generate big dollar returns on investment. But do the little things right too. Niche events will foster real relationships with customers, and provide a reason to keep the communication lines open.

(Wk 5: CRM done well—gift to ourselves)

If you made it this far, we shouldn't need to talk about commitment. Well, maybe we should talk about "commitment to an insane asylum". Many of us may not be too far from there, after the holiday season. But we shouldn't need to talk about the commitment to do what is needed to be successful.

So let's talk about funding.

Yikes. The CFO looks nervous. Everyone likes to talk about commitment. It's the money part that gets uncomfortable. Yet, we know that we can't have one without the other. The most surefire success indicator for CRM in the retail industry is funding. If we don't have the budget, our CRM program is in serious jeopardy.

When I visited Italy not too long ago, I had 2 important revelations. There I was, sitting in a sunny *piazza* at a fine Venetian *ristorante*, enjoying a little calamari, some pasta, a good Italian wine, when suddenly the first revelation came to me. A good CRM program is like a good restaurant. They both require commitment to make them happen.

That means funding.

If we want to start a restaurant, the first thing to consider is funding the structure itself. No building, no restaurant. We're not opening a food cart here. In CRM, we need a different kind of structure. Whether it's leased, in-house, or outsourced, we have to purchase a system to hold the customer/transaction data. No system, no CRM.

Next we better hire a chef—especially if you've tasted my cooking. We need an expert who can plan the menu, hopefully around dishes he or she can actually cook. When it comes to CRM, we'll need an expert on hand to direct the program. We can hire someone, or outsource to knowledgeable resources (I could suggest someone …), but there will have to be somebody who will spearhead the effort as head of CRM/Direct Marketing.

Of course, every chef needs a kitchen staff. Likewise, the head of CRM/Direct Marketing will need to hire and train a group of employees to execute CRM. The larger the retail organization, the larger the staff will need to be.

That's all behind the scenes. A restaurant also needs a well-trained front line staff of waiters and hosts to receive the patrons and provide top-notch service. It's up to the manager of the restaurant, not the chef, to find, hire and train his servers.

For us in retail, this role falls to the retail store manager. Additional functions and skills will be required for the retail staff to effectively build relationships with the customers. This means training, both for the staff that's there, and any new staff that comes along.

Of course, we can't have a restaurant without a cash register. Just as in a retail environment, the restaurant needs a Point of Purchase terminal to account for transactions. But to practice proper retail CRM, we'll need additional software to capture customer information and demographic data.

All this, and we haven't served a meal yet. It's no different in retail. We must put all of these pieces in place before we capture the first piece of information that will allow us to build a relationship. This is just the initial funding for the CRM effort. If the management team is not willing to go this far, we will never make it the full distance. Stop here! Do not pass Go! Do not make Profit!

Someone get the CFO a little linguini with clam sauce—he's looking faint. Can we at least assume that there is a commitment to these initial measures? Good. Let's press on …

No one wants to eat in a dirty restaurant. We'll need a staff assigned to the mundane tasks of cleaning, washing dishes, setting tables, and sweeping floors. And we'll need someone to clean up after our CRM as well.

It's called file hygiene. If our restaurant neglects its maintenance functions, the customers will turn away, and the health department will show up and shut us down. As retailers, failure to perform proper file hygiene will leave us with a customer database that is as good as empty. We can't **communicate**, because our customer no longer lives at that address, our duplicate files aren't merged, the phone number is invalid, and the email is incorrect.

If we can't fund the file hygiene functions, we will not be able to fulfill the rest of the requirements for retail CRM. Stop here. Do not even approach Go.

Let's say we have a well-trained staff, an excellent menu, and a clean restaurant. We've got everything in place … except customers. Ever hear of advertising and marketing? This is where the real commitment from management is required.

Unfortunately, it's also the easiest expense to cut if budgets are sparse. We can't afford to have a restaurant that no one knows about. Nor can we have a CRM program with no advertising or marketing budget.

I have actually seen retailers acquire software at a very high cost, only to wait a year to install it. I've seen others install the software, capture the data in the stores, and do nothing with it. I've even witnessed retailers outsourcing their CRM after long, costly negotiations … and then watched them do nothing with it. You can lead a horse to the wine bar, but you can't make him drink.

The only successful CRM programs are those that make the final commitment to communicate to their customers. They do it often, in a manner relevant to the customer's purchases, and using all three channels (postal, phone, and email).

And yes, they spend a lot of money doing it. Quick—someone get the CFO an espresso! CRM is not an easy investment. Nevertheless, those who spend the money are handsomely rewarded with profits, and just as importantly, customer relationships. All the other retailers stare at their empty plate and wonder why these other folks are so much better fed.

You CAN have your cake and eat it too. (By the way, I'll try the *canoli* and the raspberry *torta*). But you have to bake the cake first. That requires commitment on the part of everyone in the organization, all the way up to the top level. There is no other way.

You remember, I mentioned that I had two revelations at that lovely Venetian restaurant. The other revelation was that I really should do this more often—taking a little vacation, enjoying a good meal, and relaxing enough to have these remarkable insights into the nature of CRM.

Well, maybe the insights weren't all that remarkable. At least I had a great vacation and some very nice meals.

I hope you will too.

My Suggestion:
   Take a break. You deserve it.

Using any of the techniques referred to in *Jems from Johnson* will ensure that you'll have success in the coming years' CRM efforts. I know both you and your company will have a great year.

Just remember to:

Communicate, Communicate, Communicate.

And that....

The gem cannot be polished without friction, nor man perfected without trials.

Epilogue

Now that you have finished the *Jems* year, you must plan your next year using all that you have learned. You must go out and "do something" to enhance your customer relationship.

Building customer loyalty is not rocket science. It is hard work but it is more common sense than science. Do the things that allow you to know your customers, know where they come from, what they buy, what turns them on, and what you have to do to get them to purchase again. Allow your friendly computer to help you do the analysis that will help you pick the customers to focus on.

Start by finding out who your customer is. If you don't know them, you can't **communicate** to them. With your computer systems, determine what, when, and how much they are buying. That will allow you to segment your customers. Once segmented, you can **communicate, communicate, communicate** to the right customer with the right message at the right time.

Find out where your customers live. Knowing where your customers live will tell you where your next customers will come from. Don't waste time and money going where your customers aren't.

Along the way, build processes, procedures and systems to keep the database clean, accurate and timely. Every organization in the company will be looking for direction on customer relationship management. You will be confident in your recommendations.

Identify who the movers and shakers are in your customer database. Stay in touch with them, especially if you have more than a few store locations. Make sure the customer is aware of the locations near them as well as your web/call center facilities.

Remember, thank you is an underutilized expression. Don't be afraid to thank your customers with gifts. Your company will be rewarded over and over again for rewarding your customers.

- Customer Relationship Management (CRM) starts with the first transaction with the customer whether on the web, thru a call center or in a brick and mortar store. Make all associates accountable for capturing the information that can be used to **communicate** to the customer. It requires attention to detail every week of the year. Provide reports to identify problems and opportunities.

- Reinforce every day that the company's goal is to service customers. That can best be done if we have information about the customer. It must be accurate, timely and relevant. Commit the funds to do the dirty work of file hygiene (keeping the database clean, accurate and timely).

- Acknowledge that getting the computer system installed and populated with data is just the beginning. Now you have to use the information that can be generated to the advantage of the customer and the company.

- Sign on to the fact that the only way to motivate the customer to come back for more is via communication. Commit the funds to **communicate** using a blend of all three channels; postal, email, voice messaging.

- Thank your customers. They will reward you for rewarding them. Make the reward as relevant to the customer as possible. The more personal the better.

- Spend as much time identifying the customers you should not communicate to as you spend identifying those to whom you should **communicate**. The savings will help fund the vast amount of effort to get CRM right.

Have I stressed the importance of **COMMUNICATION**?

Acknowledgement

There are many people to thank (bear with me—this won't take as long as one of those Academy Award speeches!).

I would first like to recognize *Deb Diament.* It was she who came up with the name *JEMS from Johnson* after we learned of *Brian Woolf's* concept of segmenting customers according to their purchase history as "Diamonds, Rubies, Opals, and Pearls."

Deepest gratitude to my dear wife, *Tina,* for her inspiration in all of my endeavors, and without whom much of my work would make little sense!

I wish to thank *Eric Beall* who was instrumental in compiling a newsletter format into a real book. *Toni Pells* provided expertise in editing for which I am most grateful.

Thank you to colleagues who allowed me to use their CRM success stories as a basis for *Jems.* Mostly to *Jeff Glick,* my first consulting client, who has taken my advice and traveled to CRM heaven and actually proved that my advice isn't THAT bad!

I have learned so much in my three decades + in the retail business. As an information specialist and in retail operations and finally in Customer Relationship Management, I learned from the people with whom I worked and for whom I consulted. I am most grateful for having had this opportunity to have some positive effect on your business. You've certainly had a positive effect on mine!

About the Author

CLAUDE A. JOHNSON

Mr. Johnson is a specialist in Customer Relationship Management (CRM) for retailers. Claude is considered a visionary in the retail database marketing arena. With over three decades' experience in the retail industry, Claude has worked with hundreds of retailers to develop and implement successful customer database marketing programs.

Having served clients such as, Glik Stores, April Cornell, Bob's Stores, Chico's, Brown Shoe (Naturalizer), Pep Boys, Liz Claiborne, Bachrach, Loehmann's, Movado, Kate Spade, Capezio and more, he has been able to increase the use of CRM to the advantage of retailers, resorts, restaurants, grocers and their customers. In every case, he has generated measurable increases in sales and profits.

Claude has an impressive background, both in and out of the retail and database marketing industries. A graduate of the US Military Academy at West Point, he spent five years in the service before beginning his retail career at Lane Bryant. There and at Members Only, Claude served in an information management, store operations, distribution, and processing capacity. In 1986, he became Executive VP and Chief Administrative Officer at NBO Stores, spearheading the company's program to build its own customer database—quite possibly the first time any retail chain developed an instant customer database using information from transactions other than those of their own credit card. While at NBO, Claude created, developed, tested, and implemented the process that came to be known as Credit Card Reverse Append.

Claude served as Director Database Marketing Sales for STS Systems in Montreal, Canada. In this capacity, he supported, trained, and consulted with all STS retail clients in North America.

He was formerly Vice President of Loyalty Programs at OneCard, and was also President and Founder of Retail Resources, a database marketing service bureau with over 50 retail, resort, and restaurant clients.

Today, Claude is an independent consultant in retail CRM as well as president of KWI-CRM, a CRM outsource solution for specialty retailers. He is widely recognized throughout the retail industry and by leading industry publications, such as *Direct Marketing Magazine, DM News,* and *Direct, Stores* for his innovative database marketing vision and instinct. He publishes a free, bi-weekly, electronic newsletter titled *Jems from Johnson*. It speaks about the statistics in retail CRM, what one needs to know and then what to do with the statistics.

Index

978-0-595-42261-6
0-595-42261-6

Printed in the United States
92521LV00004B/131/A